For Asher and Noa

Contents

INTRODUCTION

The Purpose of This Book

Years ago, I was visiting a church near Geneva, Switzerland, as part of an interfaith retreat hosted by the World Council of Churches (WCC). Two dozen of us—Jews, Christians, and Muslims—were studying, praying, and speaking together in order to build bridges to end violence and hatred. We visited synagogues and mosques, and that Sunday morning, we found ourselves in a beautiful old cathedral, Holy Trinity Anglican Church, listening to the hymns and words of Christianity. When it came time for the reading of Scripture, a representative from the WCC, Dr. Clare Amos, got up to speak. As it happened, the New Testament reading that morning was Luke 13:10–17, not one that was particularly friendly to the Jews in the audience who had traveled thousands of miles to engage in interfaith strengthening workshops. The passage tells the story of Jesus teaching in one of the synagogues on the Sabbath. A woman "who had been crippled by a spirit for eighteen years" appears.[1] Jesus pauses from his teaching, calls over to the woman, and heals her. The story continues with the leaders of the synagogue crying out in indignation that Jesus had violated the Sabbath, stating, "There are six days for work. So come and be healed on those days, not on the Sabbath."[2] Jesus cries out, "You hypocrites! Doesn't each of you on the Sabbath untie your ox or donkey from the stall and lead it out to give it water? Then should not this woman, a daughter of Abraham, whom Satan has kept bound for eighteen long years, be set free on the Sabbath day from what bound her?"[3] The Luke narrative depicts the leaders of the synagogue as shamed, and the crowd favors Jesus.

With limited success, Dr. Amos attempted to distance herself and her homily from the irredeemable hypocrisy of the synagogue leadership contained in the passage. She seemed to be as disturbed that this was the passage she had been given as we Jews were to have heard it in a church that was supposed to be welcoming an interfaith cohort of discourse and understanding. True, it was a church, with its own leadership and decision makers, and no doubt the choice of reading that day was happenstance, perhaps part of a liturgical reading schedule throughout the year. Nevertheless, I found myself aghast that those in the church leadership did not speak to one another with a reminder that interfaith friends would be in the pews that day and they should perhaps choose a reading better suited to the context. I have no doubt that the leadership of the church and the WCC meant no malice in their choice and perhaps were sticking to the custom of reading the assigned Gospel passage for that Sunday. However, it occurred to me that situations like this do arise, but they can be easily fixed to avoid tension, discomfort, or worse, accidental anti-Semitism. It was moments like this one that inevitably led to the creation of this volume.

Since the beginning of my rabbinical training, interfaith work has always been one of my passions. Indeed, my passion for interfaith dialogue and education began long before I entered seminary—when I was attending Boston University. I was a psychology major, but I always had an interest in Judaism and took electives that would fulfill my need to learn more about it. I was lucky enough to be attending a university with a strong Jewish studies department that offered classes on Jewish philosophy taught by Elie Wiesel and classes beyond the standard spectrum of core classes, such as Holocaust and Music, which analyzed the Jewish music produced before, during, and after the Holocaust. It was in this class that I was introduced, by way of a guest lecturer, to the Lipper Internship of the Museum of Jewish Heritage, a living memorial to the Holocaust. The museum, located in Battery Park, New York, sponsored students in the Northeast and trained them to become docents of the museum itself. We students also traveled to schools in the Boston area to teach non-Jewish students about the Holocaust. Armed with slides, curricula, and my Jewish upbringing, I stood in front of middle school and high school students attempting to help them understand the horrific consequences of anti-Semitism. After a first session in the classroom, I would be the docent for that class when the students took a field trip to the museum in New York City.

As I sat on the express trains from Boston to New York with business commuters, I went over each exhibit in my mind and outlined what I would say to the group of students. While the Lipper Internship only lasted a year, I was not ready to let go, and the museum allowed me to come and substitute or teach from time to time. It was then that I realized I had awakened something in me, but I was unsure of what it was specifically.

Was it an interest in the Holocaust? Genocide in general? Museum work? Teaching? It was not until six years later, while studying in Jerusalem for my first year of rabbinical seminary at Hebrew Union College–Jewish Institute of Religion (HUC-JIR), that I realized it was, indeed, interfaith dialogue and education that brought me so much joy. Just a short tram ride from the HUC-JIR campus was a Swedish theological Christian seminary. After some from that seminary were invited to speak with us on our campus, we were invited to visit theirs. I volunteered to take the lead and be the liaison for this program, walking my fellow students down the cobblestone streets of Jerusalem to the Swedish seminary building. In speaking about Judaism to the excited and curious Christian students, I realized that the energy that they were exhibiting fed my own energy, and their respectful questions yielded respectful answers, humor, and joy—all discovered in our similarities and differences. I began to seek out this energy as my years in seminary continued in the four years I spent at the Cincinnati campus of HUC-JIR. Sporadically, the dean of students would receive requests for interfaith speakers from schools, churches, and other institutions around the Ohio area and would offer a first-to-email-back-gets-the-gig system. When opportunities presented themselves, I was always first in line, whether it was to travel to rural churches, teach at the local Catholic school, or host visiting non-Jewish groups. The elective classes I chose to take also reflected my passion, as I scrambled to write notes quickly in classes such as Christian Scriptures. As the time came for me to begin thinking about the topic for my master's thesis, I found my way to the faculty's New Testament scholar, and eventually, together we decided that a look at *Nostra aetate* fifty years later would be a fruitful exercise.[4]

Additionally, each summer during my years in seminary, we students were responsible for finding an internship or summer job that would help enhance our rabbinates. Each summer, I chose interfaith-focused jobs, including being a Jewish representative of the Chautauqua Institution; serving as the first Jewish chaplain at a hospital in Louisville, Kentucky; and traveling to Switzerland to take part in an interfaith seminar at the Ecumenical Institute at Bossey. My ecumenical activities were not limited to the summers, as I also volunteered to work with the American Jewish World Service and traveled to El Salvador with rabbinical students of varying denominations to help with environmental concerns. After ordination, I made it a point to engage in interfaith activities in my rabbinate in whatever way possible.

In the absence of an interfaith council at my first pulpit, located in St. Thomas, Virgin Islands, I took it upon myself to create and lead the Interfaith Council of the Caribbean, which, at the end of my two-year tenure, represented over fifteen faith communities in the US and British Virgin Islands. I also sought out board positions in non-Jewish organizations, such as the Salvation Army, Catholic Charities, and United Way. Giving a Jewish voice to the issues in the community, surrounded by non-Jews, I was able to make educational progress with those who had been sadly sheltered by only Christian understandings of religious matters.

At my second and final congregational pulpit in West Lafayette, Indiana, I followed the same path, serving as the director for the Interfaith Leaders of Greater Lafayette as well as a board member for the United Way Emergency Food and Shelter Program, the Downtown Ministers (a Christian group until my addition), the Lafayette Transitional Housing Caring Committee, the Tippecanoe County Opioid Taskforce, and the Medical Ethics Committee for IU Health Arnett Hospital. In these positions, I was able not only to contribute to my community but also to educate about language, inclusion, and threats to minority groups, such as Jews. As the leader of the interfaith coalitions that I served, I instituted multifaith panel discussions on issues facing the local community and created Thanksgiving, Martin Luther King Jr. Day, and Pride interfaith services that welcomed neighboring congregations into mine and brought my congregation to local churches and mosques. I befriended local ministers, imams, pastors, and priests; gave guest sermons and lectures at their houses of worship; and invited them to teach with me on interfaith matters or in class sessions.

The joy and fulfillment that these activities brought me far outweighed the day-to-day duties of a Reform rabbi: leading services, providing pastoral care, teaching Hebrew school, and providing Bar/Bat Mitzvah training. After the latter activities, I felt drained, tired, and anxious. Engaging in interfaith activities, no matter how long or difficult, consistently made me feel energized and alive and left me wanting more. It did not take me long to realize that while congregational work provided an outlet for these passions, I was not to be a congregational rabbi if I was to follow my true fervor in my field.

All of this, including my love for biblical scholarship, led to the conception of this book. However, the final catalysts as to developing a book proposal were the weekly (if not more frequent) phone calls and emails from Christian clergy asking questions. These ranged from what I call Judaism 101 questions to more in-depth philosophical and theological queries. Having established myself as a champion of interfaith work in each community I served, these calls and emails naturally found their way to me. These calls from Christian clergy raised questions about Old Testament verses, Hebrew pronunciation, biblical exegesis, or Christian verses with Jewish connections. Out of respect and to serve their own communities, these pastors, ministers, and priests wished to gain more knowledge of the Jewish roots of Christianity. While Christian clergy do study Hebrew and a great deal of the Old Testament in their years at seminary, these aspects are often forgotten over time, as seminary students are also required to learn Greek or Latin and a wealth of Christian theology that far outweighs the Jewish foundations of their learning. I can empathize with this, and I admit that my memory of Modern Hebrew soon faded as I embraced biblical Hebrew, Aramaic, and Rashi script as well as gained sufficient knowledge of Akkadian and Syriac. I, therefore, felt no resentment toward my Christian colleagues when they would tell me that they have sadly lost their mastery of biblical Hebrew, its roots and grammatical rules, and the like.

While these calls and emails occurred within the flurry of other communications and tasks in my rabbinate, I always seemed to find the time to answer them, and not just with quick responses but with in-depth answers that would serve my colleagues well. I recommended websites, books, commentaries, and exercises to help them. It was important to me that Christian clergy had a mastery of Judaism if they were to teach it to their flocks—not only to remove false and misleading ideas but also so that Judaism and Christianity could grow together. Even if I could not be present in their church settings, my teachings would be.

Eventually, I understood what my purpose had become in the community. Word had spread that if you needed expertise on Judaism, you called Rabbi Mike, the moniker I went by in every community. Soon I began to receive calls and emails from those members of the clergy I had yet to meet, I gathered more members in my interfaith coalition, and my time teaching on social media became more frequent. I took to writing articles based on frequently asked questions and simply began cutting and pasting links to my articles when I found posts or tweets that needed more information. After years of this practice, I had gathered enough questions and answers to create what I ultimately realized Christian clergy really needed—a handbook, something to reference when they had questions and couldn't reach or didn't have access to a "Rabbi Mike" in their own communities nationwide.

How to Use This Book

Ultimately, at its core, I set out to build a handbook that would correctly answer the questions that clergy had or address the most common misnomers that I had heard in my many talks with clergy and laypeople. I was determined not to create an addition to the "Judaism for dummies" genre. Plenty of books do Judaism great justice by outlining the basics of Shabbat, conversion, worship, liturgy, ethics, and synagogue functions. My intent was not to add to those guides, which are easily found even in the smallest Jewish sections of bookstores and libraries. Some of these books are better than others, some have become outdated, and some focus only on specific denominational views of Judaism, and tragically, these views are thought to be universally true of all Judaism. It bears repeating over and over that Judaism is not a monolith, and each author's opinion should be weighed in conjunction with others'. I humbly admit the same when it comes to my volume. No doubt there will be parts with which other rabbis and Jews disagree and other parts that may require another volume on the basics of Judaism 101 for full comprehension. Despite these possible deficiencies, I hope to spread a solid yet wide net over these topics so this book can serve as a reference, perhaps *the* reference, when dealing with Jewish-Christian dialogue and education.

In addition to these basic books on Judaism, there is a wealth of false, troubling, and conflicting information on the internet. While the internet can be a place for quick references, it is not designed to provide truthful, thorough answers to difficult questions. Moreover, while some may believe that certain questions of Judaism can be answered in 140 characters, it is simply not so. Complicated questions deserve conscientious answers. I hope this book provides such answers for Christian clergy. I want it to be a quick reference guide to which pastors, ministers, and priests around the country can turn when they are struggling with questions from their congregations about Judaism, when they wish to give sermons on certain Old Testament texts, or when they teach the history of the birth of Christianity.

With these hopes in mind, I suggest the following ways to use this volume. The first is simply to read and learn, letting that shape your own journey toward scholarship, interfaith education, and the like. It is my hope that this book can serve as a jumping-off point for new discoveries, new philosophical views on old topics, and the hunger for new learning.

Second, this book can be used as a teaching guide for adult education sessions of any size. Sections can be studied, turned into worksheets or curricula, and then taught. This book could also be used by a book club, with each participant reading and processing, chapter by chapter, the information and bringing their questions and comments to a discussion setting.

The third suggestion is to simply keep this volume on your shelf, and when a question, a situation, or a conflict arises, use it as a reference to find a solution. Ultimately, I hope this book creates less conflict between Jews and Christians not only as a prophylactic measure but also as a tool to ease tensions after mistakes have been made.

The Content

The first chapter, "Let's Right a Few Wrongs," seeks to undo the damage caused by ignorance or errors in teachings that have existed between Jews and Christians. It is an opportunity to "unlearn" what have too often become calcified and damaging misunderstandings, stereotypes, and biased arguments. This chapter intends to shine a light on the problematic sources and writings that have shaped, and continue to shape, perceptions of ancient and modern Jewry.

Chapter 2, "Avoiding the Land Mines," seeks to prevent further inadvertent conflict between Christians and Jews by identifying unlearned issues within stories, language, liturgy, and music, to name a few. Far too many Jews and Christians walk the earth believing certain stories to mean one thing when the true meaning is often hidden. In the same way, others engage in worship while being naive to the damaging words embedded in seemingly beautiful and comforting music and liturgy. This path of discernment can be hard to travel, but I hope the examples in this book can make the journey freer of twists and turns.

Chapter 3, "So Much to Celebrate," focuses on both Jewish and Christian holidays and those that can be or cannot be shared between the two. Some holidays can bring about great anxiety for Jews for reasons unknown to Christians. I describe the lines that Christians need to learn not to cross, acknowledging the still fresh wounds of fear surrounding the holiest days of our calendars.

Chapter 4, "The Difference in Our Canons," provides much-needed clarity regarding the distinct differences between Jewish and Christian Scriptures as well as dismisses notions of indistinguishable texts transcending religions. Moreover, the chapter helps show a thorough history of how both Jewish and Christian canons were created and formed and for what supposed purposes. The Bible, whether the Hebrew Bible or the Old Testament, cannot be read in a vacuum. A proper overview is needed before the books are opened. In addition to this overview, the process of how books in the canon were formed requires a critical eye, as does the way the books were translated and thus interpreted throughout the centuries.

This is where chapter 5, "Translation and Typology," comes into play. As Bishop John Shelby Spong once stated from the pulpit at the Chautauqua Institution, "The Bible did not drop down from the sky at Sinai in the King James Version."[5] While this is an amusing anecdote, it points to Spong's (and my) concern for the readers of any Bible taking the vernacular translation of the page to be complete and immovable. Rather, interpreters of the Bible must see "behind the curtain," as it were, to provide the readers with the tools to create a proper skeptical and critical reading of the holy words on the pages.

Finally, chapter 6, "Easy Answers to Eighteen Big Questions," provides a quick reference guide for many common questions asked of Jews by Christians. Admittedly, these answers are not absolute or complete—far from it. However, they do provide an overview and basic response to complicated questions that should lead those who ask to rethink the questions and follow a different path when viewing the subject in mind.

My plea, as a rabbi, educator, and Jew, is that Christians come to know more about us, about Jews and Judaism. I hope to convey a love of and appreciation for Judaism as the origin of Christianity. If Christians wish to embrace the origins of their faith and find fulfillment in the study to enhance their own religious views, this volume is a good place to start. I hope Christians will benefit from this book, but the knowledge that Christians take away from the subjects in it is of great benefit to Jews as well. The goal of this "conversation" is to create a more level playing field in interfaith discussion and dialogue. Armed with new and proper understandings, history, and a reflective discernment of language and its consequences, a Christian should feel confident entering into dialogue with a Jew, whether in formal or informal settings. In other words, Christians should know more about Judaism to make their Christian faith stronger but also to help reduce the fear and tension felt by Jews due to millennia of damage caused by the church. It is my hope that this book becomes a win-win for all parties involved.

Some Key Terms

This guide will be using terms and vocabulary Christian clergy should know for them to be able to navigate the complex subjects inside. While certain terms will be briefly defined in this book, Christian clergy should review these to make sure they feel confident when discussing the subjects covered:

BCE:	Before the Common Era, used as a secular and more inclusive replacement for BC
CE:	The Common Era, used as a secular and more inclusive replacement for AD
JPS:	The Jewish Publication Society, the most commonly used translation of the Tanakh by Jews, from Hebrew to English
Supersessionism:	Also known as "replacement theology," a Christian theological belief system that contends that the Christian, or "new," covenant with God supersedes that of the Jewish, or "old," covenant
Tanakh:	The acronym for the sections within the entirety of the Hebrew Bible—Ta = Torah (the Five Books of Moses), na = Nevi'im (prophets), and kh = Ketuvim (writings)
Typology:	The interpretation and application from Jewish Scriptures whereby an element found in the Hebrew Bible, or Old Testament, is understood to be a presage of one found in the New Testament

1

LET'S RIGHT A FEW WRONGS

Without a doubt, substantial ignorance exists in the world when it comes to Jews and Christians. Jews are, for the most part, ignorant of Christian Scripture and its origins, and Christians, again, for the most part, are ignorant of rabbinic Judaism (which formed modern Judaism). Most Christians also lack an understanding of the interpretation of Jewish Scriptures from antiquity to the first century CE. This last point, however, includes an extra step that adds an even more challenging aspect. While Jews are simply ignorant of Christian Scripture because they do not commonly read it, Christians are ignorant of Jewish Scripture not because they have not read it but because they read it through a Christian lens. We will discuss this aspect related to translation and interpretation in chapter 5. However, my purpose in this chapter is to help Christian friends understand that the view of Judaism presented through the lens of the New Testament is a skewed one, to say the least, and first-century Judaism, seen through the proper lens, differs greatly from modern Judaism.

The Gospels as a Source

To view first-century CE Judaism in its historical form, we have to do what I imagine may be difficult for some Christian clergy and laypeople: we must gently and temporarily view the Gospels in their historic contexts and recognize the human influences that shaped them. In any religion, whether it is Abrahamic or not, viewing the Holy Scriptures as "perfect"—that is, as literally handed down from God—can result in a closed-minded approach to reading Scripture and in a lack of full knowledge and understanding. I would give the same advice to those in the Jewish faith who feel that the Torah, meaning the Five Books of Moses, was written by God and is perfect in every way.

While such a literal view of Scripture exists, the modern study of Scripture provides deeper understandings that simply cannot be ignored. Working with the Torah example above, let us consider that even *if* we allow ourselves to believe that the Torah was handed down at Sinai—an unknown place in the wilderness, with thunder and lightning and the entirety of the Jewish nation there to witness it—we cannot ignore the fact that once Moses received it, it was put in the hands of human beings. The divine nature of the law of the Torah and its authority are mediated through faithful but fallible human beings. Therefore, if we follow the idea that it was handed down in a perfect form, its perfection was slowly and systematically reduced when it was transferred as oral accounts, copied by scribes, and later translated. Humans make mistakes, and it would be unfair to believe that scribes, translators, and clergy would make mistakes and errors in every instance except in handling the Torah. More relevant to our discussion, the same can be said of the Gospels. Christians view the Gospels as divinely inspired, but they were also written down, spread to others, copied and translated, and interpreted by faithful and fallible human beings. The original "perfect" form of the Gospels is not something we can recover.

For the purposes of this book, which aims to educate Christians regarding the historical and current lives of Jews, we look at Scripture not in a flattened literalistic way but in a way that uses modern scholarship to understand the real challenges and obstacles that stood in front of the Gospel writers as they described first-century Judaism and the life of Jesus as a first-century Jew. It is important for Christians to be aware of the potentially problematic readings of the New Testament and to be open to differing interpretations and questioning of historicity.

We can begin with the problem of chronology, meaning that two generations passed between Jesus's life and ministry and when the writing of the four Gospels was completed. Historically, Jesus is thought to have lived forty to seventy years before they were written. The Gospel of Mark, known to be the earliest one, is thought to have been completed in or around 72 CE. Matthew's Gospel is understood to have been written circa 85 CE, and Luke, circa 94 CE. The Gospel of John was likely the latest one, with a date close to 100 CE. While many Christian clergy and laypeople are aware of these dates, the chronological problem is not front and center.

Certainly, it can be argued (and it is) that writing about a person's life forty to seventy years after that person lived evokes serious challenges for the author. Though stories about Jesus were told orally, writing an accurate biography of any person's life years after the fact would be a challenge, even if that person were there telling you about it! As an example, I often tell my students to attempt to write biographies of their deceased grandfathers. I say, "Surely you may have some memories of him, and you may even remember clearly some stories he told you about his life. Perhaps you could dig up old birth records and photographs to help you along the way or even speak to friends or family members of your grandfather who are still alive. Even with all that, you may find the task to be difficult due to a lack of information and the amount of time that has passed." Dr. Michael Cook illustrates another example for us: "Imagine a string of beads that scatters on the floor. The odds of restringing them in their original sequence are low, and matters are further complicated if some beads have been lost and have to be replaced by new ones."[1]

The Gospel writers had very little in front of them when writing their Gospel accounts of Jesus, a challenge that still exists for Christian scholars today: "Jesus may have been an illiterate peasant (Crossan, Horsely, et al.) or a relatively learned member of the middle class (Koester, Brown, et al.); we do not know. He may have been an apocalyptist (Fredriksen) or a magician (Morton Smith), a 'wisdom' sage or a self-styled prophet. Scholars disagree on what to emphasize."[2]

Moreover, it is likely that the Gospel authors had not been alive or were very young during the time of Jesus. Their understanding of historical events and the situation in society at the time might have been limited. Would I, born in 1981, be able to give an accurate portrayal of what Jewish life was like in the 1980s based on memory? Certainly not. We are sometimes uncomfortable thinking about the Gospel writers having such limits, but the differences in the Gospels themselves reveal that each writer had unique sources and interpreted the stories through different lenses. Each was inspired in their own way, but each was also subject to human fallibility.

Moreover, while Christianity traditionally understands the name of each Gospel to represent an actual person, scholars now see the texts to have been composed anonymously, perhaps years after the persons attributed to them had died. The exercise of "pseudepigrapha"—that is, attributing a work of writing to a well-known name to give it greater authority—was not invented by the Gospel writers. Biblical books of the Hebrew Bible also carry this mark, the most well known being the books of Isaiah and Jeremiah, which "have been made by later hands, some by second- or third-generation disciples of the master . . . and others by literary editors (redactors)."[3] With a lack of any resemblance of copyright laws, biblical writers attributed the most famous and well-known names to the works in order that they would be popular and read. The naming may also have involved some symbolism: "When the Torah . . . is assigned to Moses, the Psalms to David, and wisdom books to Solomon, we should probably understand Moses as the prototype of the lawgiver, David as the prototype of psalmist, and Solomon as the prototype of a sage or wise man."[4]

Naming the Gospels after followers of Jesus was an ingenious and purposeful act. For example, take the claim that the Gospel of Matthew was written by Jesus's disciple Matthew. This gives it far more credibility than naming it after the Christian author who lived two generations later. To add to the challenges just presented, let us remember that the four Gospels were written not in the land of Israel, where Jesus resided, but likely in different locations in the Mediterranean region. Not only had time passed between Jesus's life and the time of the Gospel authors, but the writers were separated geographically from the land where Jesus lived. If the writers lived neither at the same time as Jesus nor in the same place as him, how could they give an accurate accounting of Jewish life in Judea and Galilee some forty to seventy years earlier?

I return to the example of writing your grandfather's biography: Would you know about your grandfather's adult life? Maybe. But what about his childhood? Not only did you not know him at that time in his life, but you have no direct knowledge of what life was like half a century ago. Finally, and most importantly, we cannot ignore the fact that each author, whether Jewish or Christian, secular fiction or nonfiction writer, has within them a specific agenda when writing down a story. Who is the audience of the book? Does the author have biases, conscious or unconscious, regarding the subject matter? Can any religious author truly be called an impartial one, especially when writing about their own theology and beliefs? We rely on the Gospels and other writings not for an exact historical understanding of first-century Judaism and the life of Jesus but for hints of the authors' perspectives. Could sections be true or based on the truth? Yes. But it is the notion that the Gospels reflect an accurate, unbiased historical view of first-century Judaism that creates (and created) severe gaps of ignorance between Jews and Christians.

A reader of the Gospels must understand the goal of the authors, which was to tell the story of Jesus so that, as the writer of Luke says, "you may know the certainty of the things you have been taught."[5] This "telling" did have an agenda: to present Christianity in a positive light and Jesus as the hero and the victim all at once. And when there are heroes, there are inevitable villains. The Gospels have several examples that can be read and seen as anti-Jewish in nature. This is not to be confused with anti-Semitic. The term *anti-Semitic*, coined in the late nineteenth century in Germany, refers to racial prejudice and discrimination against those who speak (or spoke) a "Semitic" language or derivative thereof. While the term *Semite* can refer to both Jews and Arabs and Semitic languages include Hebrew, Aramaic, and Arabic, anti-Semitism has come to reflect only a hatred of Jews, and new terms, such as *anti-Muslim* or *Islamophobia*, were coined to describe discrimination against non-Jewish Semites. *Anti-Jewish*, on the other hand, is not necessarily a pejorative term, though it can be. The authors of the Gospels wished to portray the stories they told as pro-Christian, intended to inspire those who read them to choose Christianity over Judaism. To accomplish this, they inevitably had to shine a negative or outdated light on aspects of first-century Judaism and present Christianity as the "correct" or "new" path. Dr. Michael Cook, a leading New Testament scholar, points out succinct examples of "anti-Jewish" choices in the Gospels. For example, he shows that the author of the Gospel of Matthew removes the "Judaism" from

Jesus's theology and at the same time "systematically intensifies Mark's many *negatives* toward the Jews."[6] The best examples of this are found in the differences in Mark 12:28ff. and Matthew 22:35ff. Cook shows these in a table:[7]

Mark 12:28ff.	Matthew 22:35ff.— revising Mark
One of the scribes . . . asked him, "Which commandment is the first of all?"	One of [the Pharisees], a lawyer, asked him a question, *to test him*. "Teacher, which is the great commandment in the law?"
Jesus answered, "the first is, *'Hear, O Israel: The Lord our God, the Lord is one; and*	And he said to him, _____
You shall love the Lord your God with all your heart, and with all your soul, and with all your mind, and with all your strength.' . . ."	You shall love the Lord your God with all your heart, and with all your soul, and with all your mind. This is the great and first commandment . . .
And the scribe said . . . , "You are right, Teacher . . ." Jesus . . . said to him, "You are not far from the kingdom of God."	_____

In Cook's chart, we should immediately see the "anti-Jewish" maneuvers used by the author of the Gospel of Matthew. Let us begin with the change in Matthew that we would categorize as anti-Jewish but not as a pejorative. When Jesus is asked by the scribe in Mark about the first commandment of them all, Jesus replies with his telling of the following words from Deuteronomy 6:4–6: "Hear, O Israel! The LORD is our God, the LORD alone. You shall love the LORD your God with all your heart and with all your soul and with all your might." These words were and are currently the "watchword" of the Jewish faith, known best as the Sh'ma. In Judaism, the words of the Sh'ma are said twice daily, before sleep, and as the last words before death. The author of Mark shows Jesus's knowledge of this by writing that Jesus answers with Deuteronomy 6:4–6 when asked the question by the scribe. There is an inherent "Jewishness" in his answer, according to Mark. However, when Matthew, using Mark's Gospel as a source, retells the story, he has Jesus leave out the first verse, Deuteronomy 6:4, "Hear, O Israel! The LORD is our God, the LORD alone."[8] By doing so, Cook argues, Matthew has removed the word "Israel," thus removing the "Jewishness" from the commandment. Again, this use of editing is categorized as "anti-Jewish" but not negative, as Matthew instead wishes to shape Jesus's answer as less Jewish.

On the other hand, Matthew does engage in a "negative" anti-Jewish edit in these verses as well. While Mark tells the story of an innocent quandary asked by one of the "scribes," Matthew intentionally categorizes the asker as a "Pharisee" and adds the words "to test him." Matthew removes the innocent notion of a question built from curiosity and describes the Pharisee as one who wishes to quiz Jesus on his knowledge of Judaism. As Cook elucidates, "It is with Matthew, then, that we first detect a disturbing pattern: a Christian writer intensifies his source's negatives about Jews and omits the positive."[9] One cannot hope to understand the words of the New Testament without acknowledging the common and sometimes obvious agendas of the Gospel writers. *This affects how readers approach the same stories as told in the other gospels.*

Moreover, history tells us that dozens of other "gospels" were written but removed from the actual canon for theological or political reasons. Therefore, it is not just the authors' agendas we must be wary of but also those of each compiler, redactor, and canonizer. Do other "gospels" provide a more historical understanding of Jesus's life or that of first-century Judaism? It was the decision of those in power at the time to decide which writings were to be considered history and accurate and which were not. This practice's subjectivity goes without saying. We will discuss this more in later chapters.

While these aspects above are certainly taught in some liberal Christian seminaries—as are other challenges, such as the fourth Q source theory—everyday Christians (to say nothing of Jews) are ignorant of them. This is mainly due to the wide gap in education between clergy and laypeople in the world of religion. While clergy are exposed to multiple authorship theories, biblical criticism, and archaeology, the average Christian may feel an obligation to uphold the authority of the texts and not raise questions about the development of the canonical text of the Bible. While there is plenty to note on the historical life of Jesus and the discrepancies found in the Gospels and New Testament, what is more concerning for us in our discussion are the misconceptions regarding first-century Jews and Judaism, which have led to, among other things, anti-Semitism and a lack of understanding of modern Judaism by Christians. We will see more on anti-Jewish roots within the Gospels in chapter 2.

First-Century Judaism: What It Was and What It Wasn't

To understand what first-century Judaism was, we must start back further on the time line and discuss the events that led up to Jews living in Judea under Roman control. The year 587 BCE saw the destruction of the Great Temple in Jerusalem by the Babylonian Empire, permanently changing the core of Judaism and its theological views. Jews of the time had a choice whether to accept that the Babylonian army, helped by its gods, had truly defeated the God of Israel and destroyed His home or to see the event as a reflection of their own sins and faults, as explained through the words of Lamentations:

Because the LORD *has afflicted her*
For her many transgressions;
Her infants have gone into captivity
Before the enemy.[10]

This became the prevalent idea within Judaism—that the Jewish God was indestructible and more powerful than all the others and any defeat was because the God of Israel allowed it as punishment. The roots of this kind of theology originate in the Torah and Hebrew Bible, but this thinking was officially cemented when the Great Temple was destroyed.

Half a century later, Cyrus the Great, the king of Persia and Medea, destroyed the Assyrians, the conquerors of Israel, and the Babylonians, the conquerors of Judah, and decreed that the Great Temple was to be rebuilt as part of his "benevolence which seemed to sit well both with his temperament and with the need to govern a large and far flung empire."[11] No doubt Jews of the time felt that the God of Israel was controlling Cyrus and that God had finally forgiven the Jewish people for their sins that caused the destruction of the temple. The Second Temple was completed in 515 BCE. The Jewish center had returned but not without some significant changes. While the vessels and other religious objects were returned from the Babylonian Empire and the altar was built in the same place as its predecessor, the Second Temple was in no way comparable to the beauty and extensiveness of the First Temple.

Following the Persian Empire, the small sliver of land on which the Jews resided changed hands several times. The Hellenistic period began in 334 BCE with Alexander the Great. With Hellenization came the assimilation and reinterpretation of Jewish culture as it mixed with Greek culture, creating "several varieties of Hellenistic Judaism."[12] After Alexander's death, his kingdom was divided between the dynasties of the Seleucids and Ptolemies. The Seleucids invaded and gained control of the Holy Land after waging war with the Ptolemies.

By 175 BCE, Jews began to feel the pressure and influence of Hellenistic assimilation, which eventually led to the Maccabean Revolt in 168 BCE. This story is chronicled in the book of Maccabees, seen as apocryphal in Judaism, and included in the canon of some Christian Bibles. While we will discuss the religious and ritual aspects of Hanukkah in chapter 3 and the choice to keep the book of Maccabees out of the Jewish canon in chapter 4, for the purposes of our discussion here, the Hellenization and forced assimilation by the Greeks led to a bloody and political uprising against Antiochus IV Epiphanes. Under Antiochus IV, Jews were no longer allowed to live under their own laws, meaning the laws of the Torah, and were considered "second-class citizens in an oligarchy."[13] While this is another story entirely, it is important to understand the foundation of politics and emotions within the Jewish mindset in the first century CE.

Following the Maccabean Revolt came the beginning of the Hasmonean period, which directly preceded the Roman conquest. More important than the military battles was the beginning of what is known as sectarianism, meaning that Jews began to see themselves as having differing ideologies under the same umbrella of Judaism. However, as Lawrence Schiffman points out, at this stage, we do not see such a strong break in sects as we do in the first century CE: "Indeed, what divided the groups from one another was only a small part of their faith and practice; what brought them together as a nation, civilization, and religion far outweighed the differences, which tend to be exaggerated in the sources, so often written as polemics rather than as objective appraisals."[14]

By the end of the Hasmonean dynasty, Rome had officially taken control of Judea, and by this point, the sects of Judaism, unlike half a century earlier, began to divide, evolving into the sects known as the Pharisees and the Sadducees. It is important that Christians or any readers of the New Testament see the Pharisees and Sadducees through the lens of historical accuracy. And what I am arguing is that historical accuracy regarding these sects cannot be discovered by reading the Gospels. As we spoke about earlier, the Gospel writers had their own agendas regarding the framing of Jewish life in the first century and how Jewish leaders interacted with the character of Jesus. As we discuss the historical view of these sects, let us keep in mind the words of Rabbi Samuel Sandmel:

> No group in history has had a greater injustice done to its fine qualities and positive virtues than have the Pharisees through parts of the Gospels. Western tradition, taking its cue from the New Testament, has accorded the word "Pharisee" with the connotation of one satisfied with the mere externals of religion, or else a hypocrite. That Pharisaism was not immune from the possibility of such aberration is attested by the Pharisaic writings themselves, which warn against it by depicting caustically the Pharisee who has gone astray. The denunciations in the New Testament, however, are not limited to potential aberrations, but to all of Pharisaism and to all Pharisees. And earlier generations of Christian scholarship, going on from these denunciations, have tended to label all of Judaism as no more than the hollow shell of religious observance, or as pure and simple as hypocrisy.[15]

Rabbi Sandmel's warning is real and necessary as we enter this phase of our study regarding first-century Judaism. Jews of the time faced dangers similar to what they face today. One of those is Christian authors characterizing the New Testament as historical fact rather than as theological interpretation or allegory. Most laypeople within Judaism and Christianity know little to nothing of the Pharisees and Sadducees other than what is written or spoken about in the New Testament. As Rabbi Sandmel correctly points out, these categorizations by Christian Gospel writers are unfair, to say the least, as is the prejudice against all Jews that derived from them. For now, let us begin with this basic description of the Pharisees:

> *Pharisees:* a group of Jews active in the period of the Second Temple. Many scholars speculate that these Jews were forerunners of the rabbis, though this view has increasingly been challenged. In any event, Pharisees, as described by Josephus and others, were known for their concern with purity and their strict observance of the Law. As represented in the New Testament and well into the modern period, the term *Pharisee* was often used in a derogatory sense by Christians, arguing that the Pharisees were indeed the Jews, with their overemphasis on the Law and ceremonies and their rejection of Jesus.[16]

As the *Companion to Jewish Studies* argues, it is important to dismiss and discard the polemical view of the Pharisees based solely on subjective views. For example, let us first examine the view of Pharisees through the lens of Flavius Josephus, a Jewish historian who is thought to have lived between 38 and 100 CE. Josephus is known for describing what he calls the four "philosophies" of Judaism in the first century CE: Pharisees, Sadducees, Essenes, and Activists. Only the first two are relevant to our discussion, though it is important to note that it is likely Jesus considered himself a Pharisee, but the Roman government considered Jesus and possibly his followers to be Activists. Josephus describes the Pharisees as follows:

Now for the Pharisees, they live meanly, and despise delicacies in diet; and they follow the contract of reason: and what that prescribes to them as good for them they do: and they think they ought earnestly to strive to observe reason's dictates for practice. They also pay a respect [*sic*] to such as are in years: nor are they so bold as to contradict them in anything which they have introduced. And when they determine that all things are done by fate, they do not take away the freedom from men of acting as they think fit: since their notion is, that it hath pleased God to make a temperament; whereby what he wills is done; but so that the will of man can act virtuously or viciously. . . . On account of which doctrines they are able greatly to persuade the body of the people: and whatsoever they do about divine worship, prayers, and sacrifices, they perform them according to their direction.[17]

While this is somewhat helpful in understanding first-century Pharisees and their basic philosophy, we must take Josephus's words with an understanding of his bias. As Gary Porton elucidates, "Previous generations of scholars accepted Josephus' claim that the Pharisees controlled the Jewish community, especially after the destruction of the Temple. However, modern scholarship has not only rejected Josephus' picture of the scope of the Pharisees' influence, but also much of the descriptions of the Pharisees and Sadducees in the New Testament and the rabbinic documents. . . . While we may accept the broad outline of Josephus' history, the details with which he fills in his account are less certain."[18]

In fact, it is important for Christians to know that all the sources that mention Pharisees, Paul, the Gospels, and rabbinic literature contain biases in their descriptions. How these are presented, even in modern writing, reflects the agenda of the author, whether it is about what they believed or how they were viewed by others at the time:

> The Pharisees were a kind of reform movement within the Jewish people that was centered on Jerusalem and Judea. The Pharisees sought to convert other Jews to their way of thinking about God and Torah, a way of thinking that incorporated seeming changes in the written Torah's practices that were mandated by what the Pharisees called "The tradition of the Elders." . . . It is quite plausible, therefore, that other Jews, such as the Galilean Jesus, would reject angrily such ideas as an affront to the Torah and as sacrilege.[19]

Pharisees were interested in text and interpretation rather than in sacrifices and the cultic rituals that were practiced by the Sadducees. In fact, it is this difference that spurred tension between the two groups, especially because the Sadducees, whose interpretations of the law hinged upon their status as aristocrats, rejected any new interpretations of the Torah by the Pharisees, most certainly those that would take the central attention from the Second Temple and the authority of the Sadducees. Moreover, the issues of resurrection and authority of the Oral Torah (as opposed to just the Written Torah) were central to this tension: "Resurrection and the revealed Oral Torah are the major doctrinal points at issue between the Pharisees and the Sadducees. Moreover, we can see how these issues might be directly related, since it is an enormous stretch—if not an impossibility—to find a doctrine of resurrection in the Torah, so one who does not hold with an Oral Torah might well be led to deny any such doctrine."[20]

When the Second Temple was destroyed by Rome in 70 CE, the Sadducees lost their power, and with that change came the rise of the Pharisees and their transformation into the rabbinic sages. Pharisees, like their rabbinic successors, were considered scholars of text, and it was their use of texts in parables and interpretation that helped shape their view of the law and Jewish beliefs. It was the Pharisees who first "devised oral interpretations beyond the written Torah text," which were the origins of what is now known as midrash.[21] To Jewish history, Pharisees are the great predecessors of rabbinic interpretation, the creation of Halacha (Jewish law), and the power of legal arguments and interpretation as seen in the Mishnah and the Talmud: "When the Jewish uprising against Rome was suppressed, the Pharisees alone survived it as an effective force in the Jewish community. By default, as it were, their program of building grassroots Jewish communities around the Law as interpreted by oral tradition stepped front and center."[22]

This transformation can be seen through the time line of teachers and their disciples during the first century CE, specifically from Rabbi Hillel, "the greatest Pharisees of the first century,"[23] to his student Yohanan b. Zakkai, "whose disciples, according to tradition, carried him out of Jerusalem in a coffin before the city fell to the Roman troops."[24] Jewish tradition tells us that Zakkai established an "academy" at a place called Yavneh, an ancient Israeli city. With the temple destroyed in 70 CE, a new kind of noncultic Judaism had to be created, and Zakkai set out to do so with his academy. Yavneh was known as a "center of Pharisaic Judaism as it developed into rabbinic Judaism."[25] The transformation to rabbinic Judaism was not without controversy, but that is a subject we will discuss later.

It is unfortunate that most Christian readers know nothing of the historic Pharisees and that Christian writings show a very different perspective. As Roland Deines, professor of the New Testament at the University of Nottingham in the United

Kingdom, writes, "Nearly everybody seems to know enough about the Pharisees to label someone else's behaviour as 'pharisaic,' but nobody ever claims to be a Pharisee himself. Pharisees are, almost always, the 'bad guys.' They are hypocrites whose outside appearance does not match their true inner nature."[26]

One example we have already seen in Matthew's adaptation (Matt 22:35–40) of Mark's story (Mark 12:28–34) about the greatest commandment. In Matthew's tale, Pharisees are lawyers who wish only to "test" Jesus to see the status of his intellect and knowledge of the law. It is a malicious view that paints all Pharisees as arrogant and doubters of Jesus's authority. While this is a passive jab at the Pharisees, the Gospel takes a direct approach in chapter 23 in what is called the "Seven Woes on the Teachers of the Law and the Pharisees":

Woe to you, teachers of the law and Pharisees, you hypocrites! You shut the door of the kingdom of heaven in people's faces. You yourselves do not enter, nor will you let those enter who are trying to.

Woe to you, teachers of the law and Pharisees, you hypocrites! You travel over land and sea to win a single convert, and when you have succeeded, you make them twice as much a child of hell as you are.

Woe to you, blind guides! You say, "If anyone swears by the temple, it means nothing; but anyone who swears by the gold of the temple is bound by that oath." You blind fools! Which is greater: the gold, or the temple that makes the gold sacred? You also say, "If anyone swears by the altar, it means nothing; but anyone who swears by the gift on the altar is bound by that oath." You blind men! Which is greater: the gift, or the altar that makes the gift sacred? Therefore, anyone who swears by the altar swears by it and by everything on it. And anyone who swears by the temple swears by it and by the one who dwells in it. And anyone who swears by heaven swears by God's throne and by the one who sits on it.

Woe to you, teachers of the law and Pharisees, you hypocrites! You give a tenth of your spices—mint, dill, and cumin. But you have neglected the more important matters of the law—justice, mercy, and faithfulness. You should have practiced the latter, without neglecting the former. You blind guides! You strain out a gnat but swallow a camel.

Woe to you, teachers of the law and Pharisees, you hypocrites! You clean the outside of the cup and dish, but inside they are full of greed and self-indulgence. Blind Pharisee! First clean the inside of the cup and dish, and then the outside also will be clean.

Woe to you, teachers of the law and Pharisees, you hypocrites! You are like whitewashed tombs, which look beautiful on the outside but on the inside are full of the bones of the dead and everything unclean. In the same way, on the outside you appear to people as righteous but on the inside you are full of hypocrisy and wickedness.

Woe to you, teachers of the law and Pharisees, you hypocrites! You build tombs for the prophets and decorate the graves of the righteous. And you say, "If we had lived in the days of our ancestors, we would not have taken part with them in shedding the blood of the prophets." So you testify against yourselves that you are the descendants of those who murdered the prophets. Go ahead, then, and complete what your ancestors started!

You snakes! You brood of vipers! How will you escape being condemned to hell? Therefore I am sending you prophets and sages and teachers. Some of them you will kill and crucify; others you will flog in your synagogues and pursue from town to town. And so upon you will come all the righteous blood that has been shed on earth, from the blood of righteous

Abel to the blood of Zechariah son of Berekiah, whom you murdered between the temple and the altar. Truly I tell you, all this will come on this generation.[27]

Again, we must remember that this "speech" by Jesus was written up to fifty years after his death, and the Gospel writer's agenda was to write a polemic against this particular group. As Jack Miles succinctly explains, "Jesus was surely one of the greatest polemicists of all time. It is thanks to him that the very word 'Pharisee' has as its second definition in *Webster's College Dictionary* 'a sanctimonious, self-righteous, or hypocritical person.'"[28]

Matthew, as well as Mark and Luke, records another story regarding the law of the Sabbath that paints the Pharisees in an unfair light:

At that time Jesus went through the grainfields on the Sabbath. His disciples were hungry and began to pick some heads of grain and eat them. When the Pharisees saw this, they said to him, "Look! Your disciples are doing what is unlawful on the Sabbath." He answered, "Haven't you read what David did when he and his companions were hungry? He entered the house of God, and he and his companions ate the consecrated bread—which was not lawful for them to do, but only for the priests. Or haven't you read in the Law that the priests on Sabbath duty in the temple desecrate the Sabbath and yet are innocent? I tell you that something greater than the temple is here. If you had known what these words mean, 'I desire mercy, not sacrifice,' you would not have condemned the innocent. For the Son of Man is Lord of the Sabbath." Going on from that place, he went into their synagogue, and a man with a shriveled hand was there. Looking for a reason to bring charges against Jesus, they asked him, "Is it lawful to heal on the Sabbath?" He said

to them, "If any of you has a sheep and it falls into a pit on the
Sabbath, will you not take hold of it and lift it out? How much
more valuable is a person than a sheep! Therefore it is lawful
to do good on the Sabbath." Then he said to the man, "Stretch
out your hand." So he stretched it out and it was completely
restored, just as sound as the other. But the Pharisees went out
and plotted how they might kill Jesus.[29]

Here the Pharisees are seen as sticklers for the law, even in the
face of suffering. They gleefully point out those who are breaking the Torah law and, according to Jesus, "have condemned
the innocent." It is Jesus who teaches the seemingly ignorant
Pharisees to see that "it is lawful to do good on the Sabbath,"
chastising them for such an exact reading of the Torah law. The
passage paints Pharisees as heartless and without compassion
while showing Jesus as not only a healer but a better teacher and
more empathetic follower of the law. Additionally, it ignores the
understanding in Jewish law, which the Pharisees would have
known, that the preservation of life and health always supersedes
the Sabbath law. Moreover, one cannot ignore that Matthew's
tale points to the Pharisees as those who would "plot" to kill
Jesus. The unending charge of deicide against Jews of every era
begins right here in this passage.

Imagine for a moment that the Gospels and stories such as
these serve as your only "historical" sources of first-century Judaism. What would be your takeaway? One need only to skim the
words of Matthew and other books to see that Pharisees—and,
later, rabbis or perhaps all Jews—are to be labeled as "hypocrites,"
those "condemned to hell," "snakes," a "brood of vipers," murder-
ers, greedy, self-indulgent, "unclean," wicked, self-serving, and
heartless. Those who take the Gospel of Matthew as history
and Jesus's words as fact run the risk of holding a negative view

of Pharisees and thus Jews in the modern era. We see this in all forms, including that of modern pastors and their teachings. Here is one example from Kurt Skelly, the senior pastor of Faith Baptist Church in Fredericksburg, Virginia: "In our modern Christian vernacular the title *Pharisee* carries a markedly negative connotation, and rightfully so. In the days of Jesus, however, they were recognized as the most fastidiously observant religious leaders of the day. I suppose there exists some Pharisee in all of us, so it's important to recognize their toxic attitudes and behaviors."[30]

It is the job of both Jews and Christians to push past this simplistic view of first-century Judaism interpreted through the lens of Gospel writers and their avid readers. After all, it was Matthew's telling of Jesus's rejection of the Pharisees that inevitably helped spur anti-Jewish and anti-Semitic rhetoric that continues to this day.

The Sanhedrin in the First Century

One of the distortions of first-century Judaism from the New Testament regards the status and power of the Sanhedrin, the Jewish high court. The word itself is Greek, not Hebrew, from *synedrion*, meaning "assembly" or "council." Importantly, Jews of the ancient world would have not referred to the court in this way but rather used the Hebrew *beit din* (house of justice). The court, or courts, of Sanhedrin during the first century is not to be confused with the Talmudic tractate that shares the same name. The tractate, or section, of the Talmud, completed in the fifth to sixth century CE, is a law code that deals with subjects that the Sanhedrin of the first century and before may have discussed. Rather, it contains far more information and legal discussions—some in theory, not in practice—than occurred in the actual Sanhedrin court, as "the Sanhedrin was invested by later Jewish tradition with an antiquity which it probably never possessed."[31] Indeed, it is useless to project the law codes of the Talmudic Sanhedrin onto the first-century court again, if it even existed.

These are just some aspects of the subject of the Sanhedrin in which the Greek sources—namely, the Gospels, Acts, and Josephus—give a false impression. The importance of this distinction is to provide Christians with a more realistic impression of the Sanhedrin and the "trial" spoken about in the Gospels. In fact, scholars today argue that "we lack proof that such an institution yet existed by Jesus' day (nor are we certain, even later on, whether and how this *bet din*—literally, 'House of Justice'— originated, or functioned)."[32]

Let us begin with the Sanhedrin "trial" of Jesus recorded in Mark 14:53–65:

> They took Jesus to the high priest, and all the chief priests, the elders and the teachers of the law came together. Peter followed him at a distance, right into the courtyard of the high priest. There he sat with the guards and warmed himself at the fire. The chief priests and the whole Sanhedrin were looking for evidence against Jesus so that they could put him to death, but they did not find any. Many testified falsely against him, but their statements did not agree.
>
> Then some stood up and gave this false testimony against him: "We heard him say, 'I will destroy this temple made with human hands and in three days will build another, not made with hands.'" Yet even then their testimony did not agree.
>
> Then the high priest stood up before them and asked Jesus, "Are you not going to answer? What is this testimony that these men are bringing against you?" But Jesus remained silent and gave no answer.

Again the high priest asked him, "Are you the Messiah, the Son of the Blessed One?"

"I am," said Jesus. "And you will see the Son of Man sitting at the right hand of the Mighty One and coming on the clouds of heaven."

The high priest tore his clothes. "Why do we need any more witnesses?" he asked. "You have heard the blasphemy. What do you think?"

They all condemned him as worthy of death. Then some began to spit at him; they blindfolded him, struck him with their fists, and said, "Prophesy!" And the guards took him and beat him.[33]

Matthew's recording of the event is similar, with a few changes noted:

"You have said so," Jesus replied. "But I say to all of you: From now on you will see the Son of Man sitting at the right hand of the Mighty One and coming on the clouds of heaven." Then the high priest tore his clothes and said, "He has spoken blasphemy! Why do we need any more witnesses? Look, now you have heard the blasphemy. What do you think?" "He is worthy of death," they answered. Then they spit in his face and struck him with their fists. Others slapped him.[34]

There are several issues spotted right away. For one, the Sanhedrin, in its time of existence, operated only during the day, never at night. Second, and more importantly, we must dispense with the idea that it possessed any real power under Roman occupation in the first century and understand that it was, at most, an ad hoc gathering of "scribes."

Despite the impression given by the New Testament, such a tribunal was considered lawfully convened only if approved by the local Roman prefect. The Sanhedrin dealt with political crimes, particularly sedition, and essentially rubber-stamped the convener's wishes.[35]

It is unfortunate that the New Testament provides such a skewed version of the power of the Sanhedrin. It neglects the fact that the high priest of the Sadducees worked directly under and with the Roman government because of its authority. In fact, it was the high priest's duty to "notice any untoward goings-on . . . and to report them immediately to the Roman governor."[36]

The most pertinent subject regarding this misconception of the power of the Sanhedrin is its ability, or the lack thereof, to consign Jesus to the cross, as "the challenge posed by Jesus to the Jewish authorities cannot have been of such significance as to warrant a demand for his execution. The Romans . . . had both a vested political interest in his death and the authority to execute him."[37]

In the Gospels, it appears that there is a straight line between the Sanhedrin and Pilate and that the scribes and the high priest themselves were able to sentence a person to death within the Roman government. In truth, the Sanhedrin, in any century, did not have the power to initiate arrests or proclaim the execution of another person. Under Roman occupation, the Sanhedrin, if even allowed to exist, had no real power to affect those living under Roman rule and law. Certainly, the *beit din* could handle functions of Jewish law, such as religious or ritual matters, deciding answers to religious practice questions or those of Halacha, but this was the reach of its power: "It had authority over Jewish life in Judea, but Romans reserved control over some areas, especially capital punishment. For this reason, and because this trial is placed on Passover when such activities would be strictly forbidden by Jewish Law, the scene is of questionable historicity."[38] Ignoring the historical reality of Roman Occupation has grave consequences.

Moreover, a *beit din* is a holy gathering of scribes and teachers; in no world would it be possible for the members therein to "spit" on an accused subject or "beat" him. For many reasons other than those specified, Jewish and Christian scholars alike believe it is clear that the Sanhedrin episode was inserted and fabricated. It should not be taken as historical in any sense, let alone as an accurate view of the power of Jewish courts under Rome or the trial and execution sentence of Jesus.

Judaism Then and Judaism Now

Whenever I sit at the tables of interfaith dialogue, inevitably an issue of confusion arises when discussing what Jews believe or how they act because of a discrepancy between first-century (cultic and biblical) Judaism and modern-day (rabbinic) Judaism. While we modern Jews carry with us elements of our biblical ancestors, the texts of the Torah and Tanakh have been discussed and interpreted for millennia, the challenges within have been responded to by modernity, and new ways to fulfill commandments have been described outside the realm of sacrifice.

As we discussed above, the Pharisees, as the only sect of first-century Judaism to survive both the destruction of the temple in 70 CE and the Bar Kokhba revolt of 132 CE, transformed into what are now known as "rabbis." The term "literally means, 'my teacher'; originally a title for someone in an authoritative position, it came to signal a member of the group responsible for development and codification of specific sets of literature (Mishnah, Tosefta, Talmud, Midrashim)."[39] Though the shift from temple to synagogue, Pharisee to rabbi, marks an important historical point for the creation of rabbinic Judaism, it is just as crucial to discuss the Jewish community outside the land of Palestine in what is known as the Diaspora, centered in

Babylonia. Unfortunately, unlike in Palestine, where we have both Christian and Roman archaeological evidence to help shine a light on the rabbinic life of Jews at the time, in Babylonia, the only sources we have are the rabbinic texts themselves, though we know certain key points, most notably that Jews who fled Jerusalem or were exiled after the destruction of the Great Temple in 587 BCE continued to reside in Babylonia. They "began their sojourn in . . . northern Mesopotamia and the areas east of the Tigris: Assyria, Adiabene, Media, and Elam."[40] And while the history of rabbinic life and academies through the Persian period is something to be studied, for the purpose of our discussion, let us move to the creation of the rabbinic documents and sources that formed modern Judaism and remain today as paramount to Jewish communities everywhere.

These bodies of work, which constitute the Oral Torah, are known as the Mishnah, the Talmud, the Tosefta, and midrash. In short, the midrash is "running commentaries on biblical texts,"[41] and the Mishnah, Talmud, and Tosefta represent "topical groupings of materials (e.g., regarding holiday observance, family matters, jurisprudence, etc.)."[42] Though once studied and repeated only orally, the collection of rabbinic work became too much to memorize and was eventually written down into large volumes. The Mishnah, a second-century CE law code, was then commented upon by the Gemara, and both were added together into a volume codified in the fifth century CE known as the Talmud. The Tosefta, which means "supplement," adds supplementary material to the Mishnah and Gemara. While legends exist regarding the Oral Torah's multiple authors, editors, and the like, "we have no reliable information concerning the processes of their creation, the forms individual passages had before their incorporation into later documents, from where editors got what they included, what they chose to exclude, or their editorial principles in general."[43] That being said, these bodies of work became the building blocks for how Judaism was to relate to and interpret the biblical writings, how any community from any time was to answer questions about Jewish law, and how to properly observe it. These works further led to medieval and later commentaries and law codes that are still observed today by certain denominations. This also began the process of Halacha, the way to follow Jewish law in all denominations of Judaism. In other words, modern Judaism is primarily based not on the remnants of biblical and cultic aspects from the Torah and Tanakh but on the interpretations and laws that were written later by the sages and rabbis regarding how to relate that material to their own versions of modern times.

Regarding Diaspora Judaism and that which was based in Palestine, two bodies of work emerged that are now known as the Talmud Yerushalmi (the Jerusalem Talmud) and the Talmud Bavli (the Babylonian Talmud), with the former being born out of Palestine and the latter out of Babylon. While the Talmud Bavli is far more extensive and accepted as a source, the Talmud Yerushalmi is still used as a source document to discuss and argue Jewish law.

As for midrash, as Porton points out, "most scholars argue the collections of Midrashim derive from the popular sermons the rabbis delivered in late antiquity. Others maintain the Midrashim are internal rabbinic creations meant to demonstrate the rabbis' expertise in manipulating Torah."[44] Whatever the purpose or origin, the midrashim became the way for rabbis to explain and interpret the Torah, in a sense answering the questions that Jews would have about the text before they were asked. As every editor and author has their own agenda, we must realize that "sages began explaining the meaning of biblical texts, and it soon turned out that there was no longer any need to change the actual words of the texts. All that was necessary for the sage was to explain that while the text might sound as if it meant X, what it really means is Y."[45] This began an "interpretive movement" that gave power to the rabbis to unlock the mysteries of the Torah and Tanakh texts and provide answers to questions and solid explanations for conundrums, discrepancies, scribal errors, and contradictions in what was understood to be a holy and perfect Scripture. James Kugel explains it this way:

> Perhaps the most important consequence of this interpretive movement was the establishment of an overall postulate about the Bible itself. These sacred texts did not consist solely of the words on the page; those words came along with a growing body of traditional interpretations. This idea ultimately came to be formulated in rabbinic Judaism as the "two Torahs," the written text of the Pentateuch and the *Torah she-be'al peh*, the "Oral Torah"—that is, an orally transmitted explanation of the Written Torah that accompanied it and was its inseparable equal. This large body of interpretations and expansions touched virtually every verse in the Pentateuch (and a good many verses in the rest of the Hebrew Bible). For rabbinic Judaism, what the Oral Torah said was what the Pentateuch really meant.[46]

Later, in order to provide authority to the rabbinic texts of the Oral Torah, the "tradition" was formed that both the Written and the Oral Torah originated from the great revelation at Sinai. In other words, at some point, most likely between the first century BCE and the first century CE, traditional Jewish thought began to assert that while Moses was writing down the Written Torah on Sinai, God whispered the words of the Oral Torah, and the latter was passed down by word of mouth until written down in the Mishnah in the second century CE. This belief is thought by scholars to have been created by the "desire on the part of the Yavnean rabbinic authorities to solidify their authority by claiming divine origin for their own traditions."[47]

In fact, the Mishnah tractate Pirkei Avot (Wisdom of the Fathers) begins with that exact legend so as to establish authority: "Moses received the Torah at Sinai and transmitted it to Joshua, Joshua to the elders, and the elders to the prophets, and the prophets to the Men of the Great Assembly."[48] The "Torah" being described here is the Oral Torah, not the Written Torah. The tractate continues with the passing down of the oral law, with phrases beginning with "Antigonus (a man) of Socho received [the oral tradition] from Shimon the Righteous,"[49] "Yose ben Yoezer (a man) of Zeredah and Yose ben Yohanan [a man] of Jerusalem received [the oral tradition] from them [i.e. Shimon the Righteous and Antigonus],"[50] "Joshua ben Perahiah and Nittai the Arbelite received [the oral tradition] from them," and so on.[51] These words continue throughout the tractate of Pirkei Avot, providing divine influence and authority to each rabbi and sage.

So what does this mean for everyday Jews and Christians when discussing their similarities and differences? For one, Christianity was and is based on first-century Judaism, not rabbinic Judaism. This means that when Christianity was formulated, its foundations were built on the New Testament's interpretation of the Hebrew Bible (which they called the Old Testament). Rabbinic Judaism's method of interpretation of the Hebrew Bible was separate from Christianity's, and thus the two streams grew apart, with Christianity using the New Testament and canons to create a religion and rabbinic Judaism using the Oral Torah as commentary on the Written Torah to create the future of Jewish beliefs. Second, at the point where the rabbis were being formed, after the revolts and destruction of the Sadducees and other sects of the time, "the Christian movement was increasingly turning towards the Gentile world, separating itself from both Jewish people and Jewish practice."[52]

It is my hope that this chapter not only educates Christians on first-century Judaism but helps discuss and discard any

misnomers about modern Judaism and its formation in relation
to Christianity.

Key Takeaways from Chapter 1

1. It is possible and necessary to challenge the theological
   lenses that Gospel writers applied to their versions of Jesus
   and his interactions with Jewish religious leaders. Providing a more accurate historical perspective on first-century
   Judaism and Christianity can open the minds of your flock
   to a broader understanding than what is read in the Gospels alone. New interpretations that lead to greater interreligious understanding can emerge.
2. The Gospels provide a skewed version of Pharisees and Jews
   of the first century and should not be taken as historical in
   many places. Your congregation should dive deep into the
   history of first-century Judaism.
3. First-century Judaism is not modern Judaism, and Christians should become more familiar with the multiple rabbinic sources that led to the changes that created all of the
   modern denominations of their Jewish neighbors. A Christian will not get a full understanding of modern Judaism by
   reading the Bible alone.

2

AVOIDING THE LAND MINES

If you are a member of the clergy—Jewish or Christian—have you ever done or said something wrong in an interreligious setting because of a lack of tact or knowledge? If so, you are likely in good company. Words have always mattered, but in this postmodern world, they are permanently etched into history through email and social media. Indeed, miscommunication is even more expansive when we look at all the forms of modern communication besides speech. Today's standard contact for businesses as well as personal use is often delivered via email or text message. By using these modern conveniences, we put our messages at risk. There is no tone of voice in email or text messaging except what the reader substitutes for our own, which causes countless issues.[1]

Face-to-face interactions raise the stakes even higher to create atmospheres of respect and understanding. Gaffes are made, and sometimes they feel unforgivable considering the context and the origin, but bridges can be rebuilt. In this chapter, I want to review "land mines," as I call them, of accidental anti-Semitism and discuss how to avoid them before they happen. Good intentions are not sufficient in these situations. Christian leadership and laypeople need to engage in some productive discomfort to build and maintain strong relationships with the Jewish people.

The Good Samaritan

I wish to begin this chapter with a "land mine" that is often overlooked rather than begin with some of the more obvious examples. Let's look at the story of the Good Samaritan, which occurs in the Gospel of Luke 10:25–37. How many Christians know the parable in full is unknown, but the phrase *Good Samaritan* has become a common and consistently used idiom in modern culture. Strangers who help others are designated as Good Samaritans, and laws that punish onlookers for not intervening during crimes are known as Good Samaritan laws. Countless organizations and hospitals are named for the main character in the story as well. But like so many idiomatic expressions, the origin and the original meaning of the phrase are lost on many.

We should begin with some background on Samaritans. Jewish tradition tells that after the death of King Solomon, the kingdom was divided into two political entities known as the northern kingdom, called Israel or Samaria, and the southern kingdom of Judah. Samaria was a region located between Galilee in the north and Judea in the south. The tales of the two kingdoms are told in the first and second books of Kings as well as in the Prophets in the Tanakh. The northern kingdom came under attack from the Assyrian Empire, led by Tiglath-pileser III, who ruled from 745 BCE to 727 BCE; Shalmaneser V, who ruled from 727 BCE to 722 BCE; and finally Sargon II, who ruled from 722 BCE to 705 BCE. It was under Sargon's rule that the northern kingdom of Israel fell, at least according to him, as he "claims credit in his own inscriptions."[2] Sargon's accounts also "speak of either 27,280 or 27,290 exiles and of the capture of chariots. . . . He also claims to have rebuilt Samaria 'better than it was before.'"[3] What is most important for the purposes of our discussion is that when Assyria captured the northern kingdom of Israel, the law of Assyria was followed, which led to the mass exile of Jews and the replacement of them by other cultures within the Assyrian Empire: "The king of Assyria brought [people] from Babylon, Cuthah, Avva, Hamath, and Sepharvaim, and he settled them in the towns of Samaria in place of the Israelites; they took possession of Samaria and dwelt in its towns."[4]

This was done in the hope of preventing uprisings. Because this was done, the members of the southern kingdom of Judah and the Jews who followed considered Samaritans to have lost their Jewish purity. Samaritans were no longer considered Jewish but another group entirely, which created great tension between them and the Jews. As Rabbi Sandmel summarizes, "The Jews and the Samaritans regarded each other as false pretenders to the ancient heritage of divine choice and revelation. The Samaritans were, from the viewpoint of the Jews, the descendants of alien tribes transported into the northern kingdom of Israel after the Assyrians had exiled the ten northern Israelite tribes from the region in the eighth pre-Christian century."[5]

With the stage now set, we can read the parable:

On one occasion an expert in the law stood up to test Jesus. "Teacher," he asked, "what must I do to inherit eternal life?" "What is written in the Law?" he replied. "How do you read it?" He answered, "'Love the Lord your God with all your heart and with all your soul and with all your strength and with all your mind'; and, 'Love your neighbor as yourself.'" "You have answered correctly," Jesus replied. "Do this and you will live." But he wanted to justify himself, so he asked Jesus, "And who is my neighbor?" In reply Jesus said: "A man was going down from Jerusalem to Jericho, when he was attacked by robbers. They stripped him of his clothes, beat him and went away, leaving him half dead. A priest happened to be going down the same road, and when he saw the man, he passed by on the other side. So too, a Levite, when he came to the place and saw him, passed by on the other side. But a Samaritan, as he traveled, came where the man was; and when he saw him, he took pity on him. He went to him and bandaged his wounds, pouring on oil and wine. Then he put the man on his own donkey, brought him to an inn and took care of him. The next day he took out two denarii and gave them to the innkeeper. 'Look after him,' he said, 'and when I return, I will reimburse you for any extra expense you may have.' Which of these three do you think was a neighbor to the man who fell into the hands of robbers?" The expert in the law replied, "The one who had mercy on him." Jesus told him, "Go and do likewise."[6]

The account begins with "an expert in the law," often described as a "lawyer" but most likely a Pharisee who decides to "test" Jesus. We should immediately be reminded of the wording from Matthew 22:35–36, which states, "One of them, an expert in the law, tested him with this question: 'Teacher, which is the greatest commandment in the Law?'" We should notice that the author of the Gospel of Matthew changes an innocent question posed by a Jew in Mark 12:28: "One of the teachers of the law came and heard them debating. Noticing that Jesus had given them a good answer, he asked him, 'Of all the commandments, which is the most important?'" The Gospel of Luke, which contains the Good Samaritan parable, follows Matthew's interpretation, posing the Pharisee as malicious and attempting to discredit Jesus, and "by testing Jesus, the lawyer takes Satan's role."[7] The Jew's question in Luke, however, differs from the one in Mark and Matthew, but the idea is the same, as Jesus responds with the question asked in those two Gospels. While the accounts in Mark and Matthew discuss the words of Deuteronomy 6:4–5—"Hear, O Israel! The LORD is our God, the LORD alone. You shall love the LORD your God with all your heart and with all your soul and with all your might"—Luke's account adds another quote from the Torah: "Love your neighbor as yourself." These words are from Leviticus 19:18: "You shall not take vengeance or bear a grudge against your countrymen. Love your fellow as yourself: I am the LORD." A similar edict appears in Leviticus 19:34: "The stranger who resides with you shall be to you as one of your citizens; you shall love him as yourself, for you were strangers in the land of Egypt: I the LORD am your God."

Jesus answers the Pharisee by telling him that his view is correct, that these two laws from Deuteronomy 6 and Leviticus 19 are, in Jesus's view, the most important commandments and should be the most important to Jesus's followers. I will note that far too many Christian laypeople do not realize that these phrases come from the Torah and believe them to be Jesus's own invention. The words of Deuteronomy 6 are still said twice daily in Jewish prayers today and are the watchword of the Jewish faith. As for Leviticus 19, it was considered by Rabbi Akiva in the first century as "an all-embracing principle in the Torah" and serves as the defining pillar of Judaism's social justice work in modern times.[8] So many assumptions Christians make

However, it is the Jew's follow-up question of "Who is my neighbor?" that brings on the parable of the Good Samaritan. On the surface, it looks as though Jesus is simply choosing people at random—a priest, Levite, and Samaritan—as characters in his parable to demonstrate that when one sees a stranger in danger or in need, one is commanded to love that person by providing help. However, the true meaning is much darker and must be uncovered to educate Christians of the anti-Jewish and now anti-Semitic rhetoric that exists in the story. The parable tells of two Jews of certain classes passing by the man: "A priest happened to be going down the same road, and when he saw the man, he passed by on the other side. So too, a Levite, when he came to the place and saw him, passed by on the other side."[9] The priest, also known as a Kohein, is classified as a Jew who can trace his lineage back to Aaron, the great priest of the Torah. It is still a status symbol in today's Jewish world, and with it comes certain restrictions of purity. It is considered the highest in the hierarchy of lineage that contains Koheins, Levites, and Israelites. The Levite is one who traces his lineage back to one of the priestly assistants to Aaron and constitutes the second highest in the hierarchy. While the reader would expect Jesus to choose an Israelite as the third passerby, he instead chooses an enemy of the Jews, who they consider to be impure and outside of Judaism altogether, a Samaritan. There are several things at work here in the parable. While some have come to believe that the priest and the Levite disregard the man in need because of purity laws, these laws only concern the touching of corpses, not those who are alive. Indeed, the priest and the Levite have no excuse for not helping the man on the side of the road, according to Jesus, except a disregard for those in need and, more importantly, a disregard for the commandment to "love your neighbor." Here Jesus paints Jews of the highest status as arrogant, uncaring, and hypocritical to their own view of the law; indeed, Jesus points to the Jews' adherence to laws of morality only in theory and not in practice. It is the Samaritan, a member of an impure tribe in the view of Jesus's audience, who follows the law to the letter, loving the man as himself and caring for him when the Jews of pure stock would not.

The point of the parable is not to praise the Samaritan or demonstrate how and why to care for those in need. Rather, it is to discredit the Jewish hierarchy and the Jews' adherence to their own laws and claim that it is the non-Jew—the enemy of the Jews, the Samaritan—who shows mercy and love to their neighbors. The parable is, indeed, an anti-Jewish polemic that can be and has been used to paint Jews as lesser than those of

Intentionally pushes antisemitic/Antijewish messaging.

the followers of Jesus (who eventually became Christians) and adds to the anti-Semitic and supersessionist views that arose in Christianity from antiquity to the modern era.

The Charge of Deicide

As I mentioned in the introduction, while studying at university, I enlisted in an internship with the Museum of Jewish Heritage, a living memorial to the Holocaust. In addition to giving tours of the museum, my duties included traveling to classrooms in the Boston area and teaching about the Holocaust and anti-Semitism in general. One of the schools enjoyed my teaching in one of its classes so much that it invited me back to lead a two-hour presentation on Judaism and anti-Semitism for the entire middle school. I introduced my section on anti-Semitism by asking an open-ended question of the students: "Why do people hate the Jews?" A young man raised his hand and, when called upon, said strongly and assuredly, "Because they killed Jesus." I was so struck by the confidence in his statement that it took me a moment to gather myself and reduce the anger and resentment I felt. As a teacher, it was my job to attempt to refute the charge of deicide against Jews to a group of teenagers. While I feel I did a satisfactory job at the time as a twentysomething college student, having studied what I have studied and knowing what I know now, I often think back to that moment and wish I could have responded differently.

Since then, I have heard this answer to the question of the hatred of Jews more times than I'd like to admit. I have heard the cries of Jewish children who return home from school telling me, their rabbi, that fellow students charged them with the killing of Jesus. I have seen the words "Christ killers" directed toward me and others on social media. But more importantly, these incidents that I have witnessed or experienced are not isolated

Christians + others use this to justify genocide.

events. Such charges have affected Jews around the globe and have led to atrocities that include but are not limited to the Crusades, the Inquisition, the pogroms, and the Holocaust. Sadly, it has become the duty of every Jew to defend him- or herself from the onslaught of charges of deicide, but I have often preached and taught that it should be our Christian friends who fight this battle with us, not because of some misguided idea of penance or atonement, but because with the large population of Christians in the world, the message would travel much farther when it is echoed by those of that faith. While I hope that Jews can teach and convince Christians that aspects of the latter's faith or culture might be offensive (this book is an example of that attempt), I have no doubt that Christians can convince other Christians far better. Therefore, they need to step up and refute the "Christ killer" charge leveled at Jews. It is historically questionable and deeply offensive to Jewish people today.

The most problematic elements of the deicide issue stem from verses in the Gospels that should be read and interpreted with extreme care. The first text is from the Passion Narrative told in the Gospel of Matthew:

When Pilate saw that he was getting nowhere, but that instead an uproar was starting, he took water and washed his hands in front of the crowd. "I am innocent of this man's blood," he said. "It is your responsibility!" All the people answered, "His blood is on us and on our children!"[10]

Christians use the same characteristics to enforce shame through total depravity, original sin, + more,

The main issue with this passage is that it depicts "the Jews as *corporately* blameworthy in Jesus' death, with this collective blame *transmissible over time*, and with Jews characterized as *inherently murderous* and deserving *punishment*."[11] As Bishop John Shelby Spong explains,

I suspect that no other verse in all of Holy Scripture has been responsible for so much violence and so much bloodshed. People convinced that these words justified their hostility have killed millions of Jewish people over history. "The Jews asked for it," Christians have said. "The Jews acknowledged their responsibility for the death of Jesus and even requested that his blood be placed upon the backs of their children in every generation." In this way Christians have not only explained, but also made a virtue out of, their violent anti-Semitism.[12]

Quite plainly, the issue is Matthew's use of the phrase "all the people" instead of just "the crowd," which is seen in Mark 15:11: "But the chief priests stirred up the crowd to have Pilate release Barabbas instead." This is what thrusts the "corporate" blame for Jesus's death on the Jews, and not simply on the Jews named in the Gospel, if indeed the event occurred as told, but on "all" Jews for all time. The corporate blame expands to future generations by virtue of the blood curse—"His blood is on us and on our children!"[13]—which does not appear in the Gospel of Mark. As explained by Christian and Jewish scholars alike, "This unique Matthean addition resulted in Jews throughout the generations being blamed for Jesus' death."[14] This idea is not a Jewish discovery but rather commented on by Origen of Alexandria, a Christian scholar of the early third century, who explains in his writings,

And he (sc. Pilate) indeed washed himself, but they not only would not cleanse themselves from Christ's blood, but even took it upon themselves, saying, "His blood be on us and on our children." Therefore, they became guilty not only of the blood of the prophets, but, filling up the measure of their fathers, they became guilty of the blood of Christ, that they might hear God saying to them, "When ye stretch forth your hands to Me, I will hide Mine eyes from you; for your hands are full of blood" (Isa 1:15). Therefore, the blood of Jesus has come not only upon those then living, but also upon all subsequent generations of Jews until the end. Therefore, now their house has been left to them desolate (Matt 23:38).[15]

This use of Matthew to assign blame to all Jews, past and present, has caused the torture and death of countless Jews over millennia. This event must be taught in a different light and context, with the clergy providing the proper historical distance and an understanding of the author's context and agenda.

The "Christ killer" motif is also seen in the parable of the vineyard—Mark 12:1–12, Luke 20:9–19, and Matthew's reworking of Mark's tale in Matthew 21:33–46. We will use the Matthew text, but the takeaway from all three Gospels is the same:

"Listen to another parable: There was a landowner who planted a vineyard. He put a wall around it, dug a winepress in it and built a watchtower. Then he rented the vineyard to some farmers and moved to another place. When the harvest time approached, he sent his servants to the tenants to collect his fruit. The tenants seized his servants; they beat one, killed another, and stoned a third. Then he sent other servants to them, more than the first time, and the tenants treated them the same way. Last of all, he sent his son to them. 'They will respect my son,' he said. But when the tenants saw the son, they said to each other, 'This is the heir. Come, let's kill him and take his inheritance.' So they took him and threw him out of the vineyard and killed him. Therefore, when the owner of the vineyard comes, what will he do to those tenants?" "He will bring those wretches to a wretched end," they replied, "and he will rent the vineyard to other tenants, who will give him his share of the crop at harvest time." Jesus said to them, "Have you never read in the Scriptures: 'The stone the builders rejected has become the cornerstone; the Lord has done this, and it is marvelous in our eyes'? Therefore I tell you that the kingdom of God will be taken away from you and given to a people who will produce its fruit."

Both Jewish and Christian scholars have been able to "decode" the seemingly innocent parable, understanding the landowner to be God and the wicked tenants to be Jews who do not accept Jesus as the Messiah, God's Son, and plot to kill him. While "Christian tradition sees this parable as a blueprint for the replacement of Judaism by the church," there are other malicious aspects of the parable regarding the subject of deicide.[16] An implicit aspect could be the idea of "Jesus' condemnation of Jewish officials in collusion of with Rome," which adds to the blame of Jesus's crucifixion on the Jews.[17] But the explicit aspect comes from these words of the parable: "'Come, let's kill him and take his inheritance.' So they took him and threw him out of the vineyard and killed him."[18]

When the parable is read through such a lens, it can be easily seen as a prophecy of the Jews throwing Jesus out and killing him, which echoes the Passion Narrative. I will note that I have taught this parable and its dangers many times to Christian audiences, and many of the students tell me they had never realized its deeper and disturbing meaning. This parable, as well as the parable of the marriage feast (Matt 22:1–14), must be stripped of its gilded innocence and taught or discussed through the lens of anti-Jewish sentiment and the charge of deicide.

Other, more explicit examples of the accusation of deicide against Jews exist in the New Testament, including this example from the Gospel of John:

You belong to your father, the devil, and you want to carry out your father's desires. He was a murderer from the beginning, not holding to the truth, for there is no truth in him. When he lies, he speaks his native language, for he is a liar and the father of lies.[19]

This passage, in one verse, casts Jews as murderous by nature by comparing them to Satan and implying that they, like Satan, wish to murder and tell lies.[20] Other passages in the New Testament, such as Acts 3:13–15 and 1 Thessalonians 2:14–16, also paint a disturbing picture of Jews. When these verses are read or taught, it is up to Christian clergy to discuss the agenda and the origin of the bias words, explaining the work of the Gospel and New Testament writers to shift the blame of Jesus's death from Rome to a common enemy of the Christians of their day, the Jews. By 70 CE, not only had the Jews revolted and been crushed by Rome, but six years earlier, Emperor Nero "scapegoated Christians . . . for a fire in Rome itself, inflicting upon them 'grievous torments.'"[21] With Rome as an oppressive force in Judea, writings by Christians would be monitored for any sign of dissent or insurrection. Moreover, the conflict between Jews and Jewish-Christians "served Rome's purposes in just such a way," as James Carroll explains: "There is perhaps something craven in the Gospels' emphasis on 'Jews' as a threat to order in the empire, as opposed to 'Christians,' and it does not mitigate the Gospel writers' responsibility for driving this wedge to note that they were responding to Roman oppression."[22]

It was, in part, for this reason that anti-Jewish sentiment is found in the New Testament surrounding Jesus's death, shifting the idea of "the founder to whom Christians traced themselves had been crucified, a Roman punishment . . . here was reason enough to invent, and emphasize, Pilate's endeavor to release

Jesus."[23] These verses and their skewed bias toward Jews must be discussed when teaching on this subject in order to attempt to contest the millennia-old practice of identifying Jews as "Christ killers."

Liturgy

Christian interpretations of Scripture also transposed themselves upon the pages of prayer books and liturgical guides, especially as the church formed. While much of this music and poetry is beautiful and has become mainstream and sometimes even crossed religious boundaries, there existed and sadly still exists aspects of anti-Jewish rhetoric in Christian books of prayer and worship resources.

We begin with the work of the second-century bishop and poet Melito of Sardis, a Jewish convert to Christianity living near the Greek city of Smyrna, modern-day Izmir. Melito is known to be not only both the founder and the source of "the theological concept of Deicide" but also the composer of a poem that led to the creation of a Christian hymn known throughout the globe.[24] Among Melito's many historical writings and liturgical poems is the work called *Peri Pascha* (On the Passover). The homily, written between 160 and 170 CE, contains these words:

> This is the lamb being slain; this is the lamb that is speechless; this is the one born from Mary the lovely ewe-lamb; this is the one taken from the flock, and dragged to slaughter, and sacrificed at evening, and buried at night; who on the tree was not broken, in the earth was not dissolved, arose from the dead, and raised up man from the grave below. This one was murdered. And where was he murdered? In the middle of Jerusalem. By whom? By Israel.[25]

This passage and others from *Peri Pascha* are some of the oldest examples of charges of deicide against Jews in poetic form. And while *Peri Pascha* is not as well known or used in the church, it did serve as the main source for what is now known as the Improperia, meaning "reproaches." The Improperia is believed to have its earliest origins in the seventh century CE. Note how the following excerpt accuses the Jews of Jesus's death:

> Because I led you through the desert for 40 years and fed you with manna, and introduced you into a very good land: you have prepared a cross to your saviour. . . . What should I have done for you that I did not do? I have planted you as my most precious vine: but you have become all too sour: for with vinegar you have quenched my thirst, and with a lance you have pierced the body of your saviour. . . . Because of you I have slain . . . the Egyptian through his first-born sons: and you have delivered me flogged. . . . I led you out of Egypt after having drowned the Pharaoh in the Red Sea: and you have delivered me to the princes of the priests. . . . I have opened the sea before you; and you have opened my body with a lance. I went before you in the column of the fiery cloud: and you have led me to the tribunal of Pilate. . . . I fed you with Manna in the desert: and you fell on me with slaps and whips. . . . I granted you the royal sceptre: and you granted me a crown of thorns. . . . I have exalted you with great strength (virtue): and you have hanged me at the gallows of the cross.[26]

Eric Werner, in his thesis "Melito of Sardes: The First Poet of Deicide," says the hymn purposely makes a mockery of the Jewish hymn known as *dayeinu*, which is sung at each Passover Seder.[27] More to the point of our discussion, the hymn that would be sung loudly and proudly in churches around the world not only speaks of the concept of supersessionism, or replacement theology, but explicitly links the death of Jesus to the Jews, with no mention of the Romans' blame whatsoever. These words of the Improperia were permitted to stay in Catholic liturgy even after the debate in *Nostra aetate*, the Second Vatican Council, which deserves its own larger explanation before we continue with the Improperia.

The Catholic Church's "Declaration on the Relation of the Church to Non-Christian Religions"—*Nostra aetate* (Latin for "In our time")—was developed by the Second Vatican Council (1962–65) and declared by Pope Paul VI on October 28, 1965. Though it contains general comments and concerns about the Catholic Church's relationship to all non-Christian religions, a large portion of it deals specifically with the Jews.[28]

Within the section that speaks specifically about the Jewish people, the document addresses the deicide charge against them. At the time, this charge of deicide was a heavily debated point. After much discussion, the word *deicide* was omitted from the document entirely, but the message remains clear: only a small group of Jews should be held responsible for the death of Jesus rather than all Jews for all time. The section also argues against claims of supersessionism, stating that "although the Church is the new people of God, the Jews should not be presented as rejected or accursed by God."[29] It then concludes with a general polemic against persecution in general and that the church rejected anti-Semitism and acts of it "at any time and by anyone."[30]

One of the changes made by *Nostra aetate* involves a passage that once followed the Improperia but was removed from liturgy for obvious reasons:

Let not the Jew say: we did not kill Christ. For they submitted him to Pilate as judge, so that they seemed almost absolved from his death. For when Pilate said to them: You kill him, they replied: we are not permitted to kill anybody. They wanted to shift the infamy of their foul deed to a human judge; but did they deceive God, the divine judge? Whatever Pilate did, and wherein he was committed, he was to a degree an accomplice; yet in comparison with them, he was much less culpable . . . etc. (Transl. E. W.).[31]

The passage above, composed by Saint Augustine, was removed at the Second Vatican Council by Pope John Paul, but it should be noted that the Second Vatican Council occurred in 1962, meaning the writing of Melito had many centuries to take hold in Catholicism and Christianity as a whole.

A prayer that extends beyond Catholicism and into the Church of England (as well as other smaller denominations) is "For the Conversion of the Jews," which is said traditionally for Good Friday liturgy. The Catholic version is as follows:

Let us pray also for the Jews, that the Lord our God may take the veil from their hearts and that they also may acknowledge our Lord Jesus Christ. Let us pray: Almighty and everlasting God, You do not refuse Your mercy even to the Jews; hear the prayers which we offer for the blindness of that people so that they may acknowledge the light of Your truth, which is Christ, and be delivered from their darkness.[32]

Discussion of and debate on this prayer continued as late as the time of Pope Benedict XVI (served 2005–13), who, in response to an outcry against removing it from the Catholic liturgy, revised it to read,

We pray for the Jews. That our God and Lord enlighten their hearts so that they recognize Jesus Christ, the Savior of all mankind. Let us pray: Eternal God Almighty, you want all people to be saved and to arrive at the knowledge of the truth, graciously grant that by the entry of the abundance of all peoples into your Church, Israel will be saved. Through Christ our Lord.

The revision does little to erase the ideas of replacement theology and that Jews should and must be converted to Christianity and "saved" from damnation. Considering that the prayer is said on Good Friday, the day that commemorates the crucifixion of Jesus, we can see the malicious intent is not terribly subtle. This is another example of how "*Nostra Aetate* read[s] . . . like a post-Shoah attempt to dissociate the Church from the diabolical effects of its own teaching without really addressing the problem of that teaching."[33] Moreover, in 2007, when Pope Benedict made the pre–Second Vatican Council liturgy available to the public, it contained numerous anti-Jewish and anti-Semitic words and prayers. In response to the outcry from Jews around the world, Benedict states in his *Summorum Pontificum* that "what earlier generations held as sacred, remains sacred and great for us too, and it cannot be all of a sudden entirely forbidden or even considered harmful."[34] This view speaks to the unwillingness of the Catholic Church to admit that the anti-Jewish rhetoric in pre– (or post–)Second Vatican Council liturgy needs to be addressed.

As for the Church of England, the prayer for Good Friday occurs in the Book of Common Prayer, most notably in the 1662 version:

Merciful God, who has made all men, and hatest nothing that thou hast made, nor desirest the death of a sinner, but rather that he should be converted and live: Have mercy upon all Jews, Turks, Infidels, and Hereticks, and take from them all ignorance, hardens of heart, and contempt of thy Word; and so fetch them home, blessed Lord, to thy flock, that they may be saved among the remnant of the true Israelites, and be made one fold under one shepherd, Jesus Christ our Lord; who liveth and reigneth with thee and the Holy Spirit, one God, world without end. Amen.[35]

This prayer is one of fifty occurrences within the Book of Common Prayer—whether it is in England, Ireland, Canada, or the United States—that invoke the idea that Israel needs to be "saved" or "converted." While the prayer remained in the 1962 version, it was not until 2019 that the Canadian Anglican Church voted to replace the passage with one entitled "For Reconciliation with the Jews." It reads,

O GOD, who didst choose Israel to be thine inheritance: have mercy upon us and forgive us for violence and wickedness against our brother Jacob; the arrogance of our hearts and minds hath deceived us, and shame hath covered our face. Take away all pride and prejudice in us, and grant that we, together with the people whom thou didst first make thine own, may attain to the fulness [*sic*] of redemption which thou hast promised; to the honour and glory of thy most holy Name. *Amen*.[36]

It deserves repeating that the Canadian Anglican Church did not have the votes to replace the prayer entitled "For the Conversion of the Jews" with "For Reconciliation with the Jews" until 2019. It serves as a prime example of the calcified anti-Jewish and anti-Semitic sentiments that still lurk within denominational prayer books worldwide.

It is incumbent upon Christian clergy and laypeople to discover and acknowledge that the words in prayer books that charge Jews with deicide or that consider them to be targets for conversion are harmful. These passages and prayers continue to instill anti-Jewish and anti-Semitic sentiments around the globe. While it may be difficult to let go of or change traditions, each religion must, at a certain point, push past the comfortability and make the steps necessary to match the morality and viewpoint of the modern era. As Rita Ferrone summarizes,

> The Church cannot afford to treat anti-Jewish bias in the extraordinary form lightly or in a piecemeal fashion, pretending that it does not exist or assuming that it is not a problem. Anti-Jewish liturgical texts are unacceptable today and will be a continuing source of confusion and embarrassment for the Church if the difficulties they present are not addressed in a straightforward and comprehensive manner.[37]

As we end this section, I am reminded of a story told by Susannah Heschel, the daughter of the famous rabbi Abraham Joshua Heschel and an accomplished author in her own right, regarding when she visited Germany in 1986 for an interfaith gathering. During the conference, Heschel asked for a short service to honor the participants by gathering in prayer. Heschel recalls,

> I suggested to the organizers that we again close with a short service. They agreed, and proposed that we read together the "Lord's Prayer." I objected, and was told "but after all, it's a Jewish prayer." I said I would refuse to participate, and the conference chairperson asked, "Do we have to throw away our Christianity whenever we have an ecumenical service?" The local pastor intervened, suggesting we each read a psalm, in German and in Hebrew.[38]

It is important to remember that at the time, Heschel stood in Germany, the birthplace of Nazism and the creators of Auschwitz-Birkenau, Treblinka, and Sobibor. Even in the presence of a Jew, at an interfaith gathering to build understanding and reconciliation, the chair of the conference still expressed resentment about having to change his Christian traditions in response to the discomfort of this non-Christian in the audience. This attitude, shared by many Christians around the world, impedes the editing and reworking of prayers and liturgy. It also raises the issue of the appropriate times to do these prayers, which we will discuss further in the next section.

Language

In traditional Christian thought, what is the proper way to end a spontaneous prayer? Many Christians use the phrase "In Jesus's name, I pray." It is a beautiful Christian end to a Christian prayer. However, how should one end a spontaneous prayer when in a mixed religious audience? Christians need to be aware that they may inadvertently bring discomfort and feelings of isolation to non-Christians in various settings. Spontaneous prayers are incredibly powerful, both in Judaism and in Christianity, and when proper language is used in ecumenical or interfaith settings, a spontaneous prayer could be indistinguishable to either faith. However, most Jews have plenty of stories about when such care with language was not extended in their presence. I myself have many stories of the kind, ranging from prayers before middle school basketball games to an interfaith Martin Luther King Jr. Day service just years ago.

I do want to say that if your audience is all Christian, there is no need to adapt the language of your prayer; no doubt Jews use their language and rubrics for prayer when with other Jews. It is when you, as a Christian, find yourself surrounded by people of many faiths or when praying with one person of a different faith that an adjustment must be made. The replacement of "In God's name" for "In Jesus's name" is one of the simpler and more explicit adjustments we ask Christian clergy and laypeople to adopt. And there are other options that are a bit more subtle.

A term that I use frequently in my own interfaith discussions is *Christianese*. I cannot take credit for this word, which is used by others and defined on the internet as "the contained terms and jargon used within many of the branches and denominations of Christianity as a functional system of religious terminology."[39]

The term is much more easily explained through the use of examples. For instance, when I was fulfilling my first unit of clinical pastoral education (CPE) in a hospital in Kentucky, my supervisor used the word *grace* in a teaching session. Not wanting to be embarrassed, I kept quiet until I was able to meet with her alone, when I professed that I had no idea what that word meant. The conversation grew to that of how she could be more sensitive to non-Christians in her use of language.

I was happy to empathize with my CPE supervisor in her struggle with Christianese because I, as do many Jews, sometimes find myself speaking Judaese (a term whose definition is not easily found via the internet), meaning I sometimes sprinkle Hebrew words or Yiddish in my speech. In both cases, whether a speaker uses Christianese or Judaese in a mixed gathering, the result is the same: someone will feel isolated, excluded, and disrespected.

However, in educational settings and "learning moments," Jews and Christians may find it fun to teach one another about their particular languages of faith through translation. For example, a phrase in Christianese is "If it be God's will," which comes from the book of James 4:15: "If it is the Lord's will, we will live and do this or that." The definition there is somewhat clear, but the phrase is also defined, as one comedic writer puts it, as "a spiritual sounding addition to prayer. It indicates that you don't *really* think God is going to answer your prayer. Use this phrase a lot, it'll save you a lot of disappointment."[40] In the same humorous vein, I would tell Christians that rabbis often add the Hebrew phrase *Kein yehi ratzon*, which means "May this be God's will." The humor part comes in when one learns that in rabbinic circles, it has become so cliché to say *Kein yehi ratzon* at the end of sermons that the majority of rabbis will no longer do so unless attempting an inside joke with other rabbinic colleagues. Unfortunately, not all interactions between these two languages can be as rosy.

Fighting the urge to use our religious languages in mixed settings is difficult for two reasons. The first is that we become so used to speaking that way (this is especially true of clergy) that it slips out subconsciously, and we do not realize we have made a mistake until someone points it out. The second is that we sometimes become attached to the particular liturgical rubrics or speech patterns of our faith because they may shape our identities, bring us pride, or distinguish us from those around us. At times, the second reason is less easily resolved. Once, when I was preparing to introduce a Christian pastor as a speaker in my synagogue, I read the words "follower of Christ" in his bio. I did not feel comfortable saying the word "Christ" in a Jewish house of prayer, as it denotes a belief in Jesus as the Messiah, and I therefore made the difficult choice to leave those words out. A few days later, when meeting with the pastor, he expressed how insulted he was by my action, since being a "follower of Christ" was a major element of his identity. Situations like this are not easily resolvable, but they can be. It simply takes the difficult work of breaking through our own comfortability and attempting to make sure no one crosses a line of integrity. It is a delicate but necessary balance. The use of Christianese can feel exclusionary to Jews or non-Christians, whether used in everyday speech, prayer, or teaching sessions. Acting on this awareness may be difficult for Christian clergy or even devoted Christian laypeople, but the rewards far outweigh the price.

When listening to any historical documentary, lecture, or video that mentions antiquity, I and other Jews, I am certain, listen for how the transition to the first century CE is described by the speaker. For far too long, it had become commonplace for members of any society with Christian influence to speak of history through the lens of BC, which stands for "before Christ," and AD, which stands for "anno Domini," Latin for "in the year of the Lord" (as opposed to "after death," for which schoolchildren once convinced me it stood). It is surprising to me that many do not notice these terms as an invasive Christian theology placed upon secular history. Imagine learning history in school and your teacher refers to times before the first century as BC and after as AD. The words "before Christ" carry a heavy theological burden, with *Christ* being the Greek word for "Anointed One," representing a Christian version of the Messiah. "Anointed one" is the translation of the Hebrew *Mashiach* in Judaism, but more importantly, Christianity and Judaism have within them two distinct definitions of the Messiah. Christians believe that the "Messiah," according to their theology, "conforms to the incarnate supernatural dying and rising Savior-deity, second person of the Trinity, bringing immortality to individuals who 'believe in him,'"[41] and/or "presuming themselves trapped in Sin, [they] believe they will benefit vicariously from his death and resurrection and from the sacraments that reenact those pivotal events."[42]

Jews do not identify the Messiah this way. In other words, the term *Christ* (as well as the term *Mashiach*, for that matter) denotes a distinct and unique definition of the Messiah and is not a common term that can be shared by Judaism and Christianity alike. Therefore, when a Jew is in an assimilated secular world and hears "BC," they are immediately excluded and isolated, as this denotes the idea that the entire world's history revolves around the Christians' belief in their Christ. The same is true of AD, "in the year of the Lord" or "in the year of our Lord." A Jew might ask "Whose Lord?" and would staunchly disagree that they are living in a year of Jesus, the Christian "Lord."

Jews and other non-Christians have their own calendars and events that help separate certain eras from others. Jews, for example, use a Hebrew calendar, in which the year 2022 is 5782. However, as assimilated Jews, it became far easier to use the BC/AD calculation and accept it as a relatively universal system for dating historical events. The challenge then was how to make a universal system truly universal. The substitution of BCE and CE for BC and AD became the solution, and thankfully, more and more are adapting to this more respectful, more inclusive terminology. Although certain Christians may believe that using the terms *BC* and *AD* is an expression of their faith, I would note that, while this is true, the benefits of including all around you far outweigh the cost of using the specifically Christian language terms.

Music

Interfaith weddings are becoming more and more commonplace in this postmodern world, despite the pushback from fundamentalist denominations of both Judaism and Christianity. Most liberal or progressive denominations welcome interfaith families, and most clergy of those sects and their governing bodies not only support them but have special liturgy to use during marriage ceremonies and the like. As a Reform rabbi, I am proud to have officiated many interfaith weddings where either the groom or the bride was Christian. There are several handbooks and guides for clergy on either end of the spectrum to help them find a balance without betraying the integrity of values and respecting traditions.

However, a lesser-known aspect of planning in interfaith marriages is the subject of music. Surprisingly, several possible land mines surround music in all interfaith situations. Thanks to movies and television, most of us are familiar with Richard Wagner's "Treulich geführt," translated as "Bridal Chorus," though few would know it by its official name. More likely, it is known as "Here Comes the Bride." It is, no doubt, the most played (or overplayed) bridal entrance music for Christian or even secular weddings. But one will never hear this tune when attending a Jewish wedding, interfaith or not. It has become commonplace to label Wagner as "Hitler's favorite composer," though this is untrue, as "Hitler preferred Bruckner to both Wagner and Beethoven and took the idea of a 'Twilight of the Gods' rather personally. . . . Still, Wagner provided much of the Third Reich's background music, and not without an underlying affinity."[43] The latter aspect cannot be overstated, nor can Wagner's "family's friendship with Adolf Hitler."[44] This alone might be enough for the State of Israel to ban Wagner's music (which it has) or for Jewish spouses to ask to avoid Wagner's music at celebrations, including weddings, at the very least for the sake of their Jewish grandparents. However, besides Hitler's supposed love for it, there is a far more problematic element to Wagner's music:

Despite his death in 1883, two years before the birth of Hitler, he is associated with Nazism after Hitler repeatedly glorified his works. Wagner was also personally guilty of anti-Semitism: his essay "Das Judenthum in der Musik" ("Jewishness in Music"), also known as "Judebthum in die Musik" ("Judaism in Music"), attacks Jews in general and some Jewish composers in particular.[45]

A prime example of this would be how Wagner viewed Judaism as what was "wrong" with Christianity: "What was bound to prove [the Church's] ruin, and lead at last to the ever louder 'Atheism' of our day, was the tyrant-prompted thought of tracing back this Godliness upon the cross to the Jewish 'Creator of heaven and earth,' a wrathful God of Punishment who seemed to promise greater power than the self-offering, all-loving Savior of the Poor."[46] He is also quoted as saying he felt Judaism had very little to offer by way of music:

> The only musical expression his own people can offer the Jewish composer is the ceremonial music of their worship of Jehovah: the synagogue is the only source from which the Jew can draw popular motifs for his art which are intelligible to himself. However sublime we may care to imagine this musical religious service in its pure form, we cannot fail to notice that it has not come down to us in its purity. For thousands of years, it has not continued to evolve naturally. Like everything connected with Judaism, it has retained a fixed form.[47]

In addition, some may accuse Wagner of being "guilty by association" because of the use of his music at Hitler's parties and in the concentration camps of World War II. Certainly, there are ethical issues surrounding the State of Israel's decision to ban Wagner's music, as there are regarding Judaism's distaste for his music for all the above reasons. In this world of what is known as "cancel culture," no matter your political views on the subject, there are arguments to be made. However, the subject of Wagner far predates the current phenomenon, and the Jewish contempt for Wagner is quite different from that of those who have refused to see Mel Gibson's movies after his DUI and arrest in which he stated on the record, "The Jews are responsible for all the wars in the world."[48] It is also different from those who would "cancel"

Bill Cosby's honorary degrees because of multiple and proven accusations of rape or refuse to buy Harry Potter novels after J. K. Rowling's antitrans comments on Twitter. While it is easy to see the similarities and brush off the concerns of Jews regarding Wagner (and other composers) as oversensitivity or indulging in "cancel culture," I would offer the suggestion that Christian clergy and laypeople give the subject pause. True, Wagner died two years before Hitler was born, but this did not stop Hitler or the Nazi regime from adopting Wagner's music as their anthem. While Wagner, who was unapologetically anti-Semitic himself, bears no responsibility for the crimes of humanity against the Jews in Europe in the twentieth century, his music is a painful reminder for Holocaust survivors who heard the music in the concentration and death camps and thus for their children and grandchildren who heard the tales of horror that the Jews endured.

In sum, the thoughtfulness that Christian clergy should display regarding classical music in working with Jews is not an element of "cancel culture." Rather, it is a sensitivity to the fact that this composer's music was used to push the agenda of Nazis, white nationalists, and those who committed genocide. It takes little effort to google composers whom Christians adore or would like to use at interfaith events (including weddings) and see if perhaps the person behind the music was of sound character or if his or her music became an anthem for deeds of antagonists or enemies of the Jews. While Wagner is the best example for the purposes of our discussion, the warning and suggestion expands far wider, and simple steps of preparation could avoid unneeded tension.

Proselytization

When living on the island of St. Thomas in the US Virgin Islands, my wife was once greeted by six Jehovah's Witnesses when she was with our son at a playground. They approached her with a hearty "good morning," to which she politely responded in kind. As a *rebbetzen*, she was no stranger to evangelists and door-to-door proselytizing, so she handled herself quite well. One of the Jehovah's Witnesses asked if she'd like a "magazine" that featured "the greatest gift to the world." She politely declined. The young man then asked, "Are you sure? It has the greatest gift to the world, Jesus Christ." She again politely declined. The young man asked *again* if she would just take the magazine. She again politely declined and wished them a good day. Finally, they departed. Interactions like this are, sadly, a part of every Jew's life at some point. No doubt any Jew can share a similar situation. I myself have been approached by missionaries of many denominations of the Christian faith, with some being polite and some being aggressive, insulting, and threatening. While Jewish people recognize that the conversion of the world to Christianity stands as one of its major tenants, it is still a foreign concept, as Jews have not actively proselytized since the practice was outlawed by Christian-controlled Rome. Books have been written by Jews and rabbis, some of whom are colleagues, that provide strategies to push back against missionary claims, ideas of "proof texts," and threats of hell or eternal damnation. However, our discussion in this chapter is not about the above, though I believe every Christian should be aware of the Jewish arguments against missionary claims. Rather, it is a land mine that is often stepped on by those with good intentions but nevertheless must be avoided. One might ask, What are these good intentions? It was explained to me, incidentally by a Muslim colleague, this way: "Imagine that the entire world has a disease that's curable, and all people need to do is take this shot, then they'll be healthy. Wouldn't you fight hard to make sure everyone got that shot?"

When hearing it that way, the missionary intention does seem good, until one pulls apart the metaphor. This seemingly positive promise of an easy cure comes to the negative implication that those who push this intention are describing *my* religion, *my* way of life, as a disease, as unhealthy, as a pathogen, as something that can be cured. There is nothing more dehumanizing, arrogant, or insulting than to label a person, certainly a stranger, as ill because of who they are. It is incumbent upon Christian clergy and laypeople to move away from this view and remember that Jews are not broken, sick, or unfulfilled. We fear no eternal damnation, as our religion does not believe in such a thing. We needn't be convinced by "proof texts" that "predict" Jesus in our own Hebrew Scripture, because we know that Jesus's name is never mentioned and that it is improper for a Christian to tell a Jew that the former knows the correct interpretation of Jewish text better than the latter. Proselytizing is immoral and should be taught as such. I recognize that this may be difficult for some devout Christians who believe themselves to be messengers of their god, charged with the task of bringing "all to Christ," but I would remind those Christians that Jesus preached humility and to love one's neighbor. You cannot love your neighbor if you see their way of life as a disease.

In addition to direct proselytization, I have become acquainted with a related practice called "witnessing." A Christian colleague of mine explained that "witnessing" is not directly approaching someone and urging them to convert; rather, it is simply speaking about how great Jesus is and how their lives have been fulfilled in Christianity. In other words, the person "witnessing" does not directly ask or tell the Jew to convert;

instead, they simply explain to the Jew that Christianity has fulfilled their life and made their life better, and so they wish to share that with those around them. While some may appreciate this "lighter touch," I admit that I find it especially insidious. When my colleague finished explaining "witnessing," I began to think of a beer or soda commercial. In such a commercial, the actor does not stand, face the camera, and tell us, the viewers, "You should drink this; it's delicious." More often than not, it simply displays the actor drinking the beer or soda and enjoying themselves in life. They are surrounded by elements of happiness, which seem to accompany them when drinking the product, whether those elements be beautiful women, a happy family, or best friends out on the town. One need only sit in a marketing class to understand the strategy of commercials like this; they attempt to convince the human brain to think, "Hmm, with this beverage, I can be happy." In other words, "witnessing" is simply proselytization with a better marketing pitch.

Regardless of the modern attempts at evangelism, too often Jews raise alarms when approached by missionaries or those who seek to convert them, as history has told far darker stories of exile, forced conversion, torture, and murder all under the shadow of the cross. There are wonderful ways to live life as a Christian without exerting energy attempting to get your Jewish friend to try lobster.

Key Takeaways from Chapter 2

1. The parable of the Good Samaritan should be taught to your congregation with a clear and nuanced understanding. Care should be taken to avoid lifting up the Samaritan, now used as a common idiomatic expression of charity and good deeds, as the good example and the Jewish characters as the

bad. The parable contains within it anti-Jewish rhetoric and will be taken as so by Jewish listeners. Teaching your congregation to be sensitive to this issue will help strengthen Jewish-Christian relations.

2. The charge of deicide against Jews is a real source of fear for them in the modern era. The fact that they have endured and still endure anti-Semitism and violence based solely on the transmissible and corporate blame for Jesus's death should be more than enough for Christian clergy to deter their congregations from thinking this way and provide a more academic approach to these problematic texts.

3. Christian clergy should review passages and prayers from their current prayer books to see if they contain anti-Jewish or anti-Semitic rhetoric, which may include but is not limited to blame for Jesus's death on the Jews, a hope to convert Jews specifically, and replacement theology perceiving Judaism as old and insufficient.

4. Language is a powerful tool. When in a mixed audience, avoid the use of "Jesus" or "Christ" and substitute "God" instead in prayers or in speech. Be careful to exclude or explain any words that are Christian in origin to make others feel included. This is a powerful lesson to teach your congregation.

5. Certain composers of the nineteenth and twentieth centuries are stained with marks of virulent and unapologetic anti-Semitism and racism; others have had their music adored by dictators and proprietors of genocide. Reviewing the musical choices for weddings or other interfaith gatherings beforehand is an easy strategy for avoiding unwanted agitation between Jews and Christians.

6. Proselytization is immoral and insidious. Jews have endured great pain throughout history from Christians converting

many by force or subterfuge. The bloodstains on the cross are those of Jews who have suffered from the violence and torture by our Christian neighbors. This is enough reason to teach your congregation to retire the practice of proselytization and rather accept Jews and their identity as sufficient.

3

SO MUCH TO CELEBRATE

One of the bridges that can be built between Jews and Christians is that of our holidays. Many of the Christian celebrations are based, at least in part, on the Jewish holidays that preceded them, and while there are some lines that should not be crossed (and too often are), there is much to gain by discussing the similarities. This process not only will bring about a fuller understanding of the origin of Jewish holidays to Christians but will provide Jews with a better perspective on the changes that Christianity went through to evolve into its own path. The purpose of this chapter is to discuss those similarities and differences and ensure that the most information is being presented to our Christian friends about the holidays to avoid misunderstandings and missteps.

Passover

Each spring, Jews everywhere sit around their tables with family and friends to observe the Passover Seder, reenacting the exodus from Egypt as prescribed by the sages. The Passover Seder, in its form we recognize today, was a rabbinic creation modified and added to in the centuries after the destruction of the Second Temple in 70 CE. Jews, descendants of the Israelites, use this ritual to remember the story of the exodus, our journey from slavery to freedom, and with every generation, we find parallels to metaphorical journeys and social justice causes. It is a truly joyous time, a time of observance, of family and friends, and of Jewish commitment. Basics on the Passover Seder can be found in any Judaism 101 book, explaining the objects on the Seder plate, the symbolism of unleavened bread, and the many forms of the haggadah, the book that outlines the Seder and is read all evening. The rules of the Seder were and are outlined in the Talmud, our sixth-century law code within the tractate called Pesachim. *Pesach* is the Hebrew word for "Passover," coming from this verse: "And the blood on the houses where you are staying shall be a sign for you: when I see the blood I will *pass over* you, so that no plague will destroy you when I strike the land of Egypt."[1] The verse refers to the "destroyer," more commonly known as the "angel of death," who *passed over* the houses of the Israelites during the final plague in the exodus story.

Christians, as are all people, are welcome to the Seder table, as the words "Let all who are hungry come eat!" appear at the beginning of every haggadah. Jews welcome Christians and any strangers to observe this ritual and join in on the festivities with no agenda, simply welcoming friends to the table for a holiday and meal. It is and should be a time of interfaith gathering, a focus on social justice regarding the topics of global poverty, modern-day slavery, and other "plagues" within our world that transcend the attention of one religion or denomination.

However, throughout the centuries, especially in modern times, Jews too often have found the Passover Seder misrepresented or co-opted by Christians. The season that surrounds Passover is familiar to Christians, as this is their time to celebrate Good Friday and Easter, which, because of the connection to the lunar calendar, fall within the Passover week. While we can speak about the atrocities instigated by Christians against Jews that have occurred over millennia—such as pogroms and state- or church-sponsored torture and mass murder due to the charge of deicide against Jews, which we discussed in the previous chapter—the modern-day challenge is quite different. However, the pain Jews have experienced over the centuries, wherein they have faced danger and death from Christians because of the horrendous blood libel, the medieval mythology that claimed Jews kidnapped and killed Christian children for their blood (supposedly to use in the baking of Passover matzah) does bear repeating for our discussion:

> The first ritual murder charge took place in Norwich, England, in the twelfth century. A boy named William was found dead in the woods outside of town, and a monk, Thomas of Monmouth, accused local Jews of torturing him and murdering him in mockery of the crucifixion of Jesus. Although many townspeople did not believe this claim, a cult venerating the boy eventually sprang up. At this time the myth began to circulate that each year, Jewish leaders around the world met to choose a country and a town from which a Christian would be apprehended and murdered. . . . The blood libel spread throughout the Christian world in the Middle Ages. When a Christian child went missing, it was not uncommon for local Jews to be blamed. Even when there was no evidence that any Jew had anything to do with the missing child, Jews were tortured until they confessed to heinous crimes.[2]

For centuries, Jews have been understandably wary of their Christian neighbors around Passover and Easter for fear of a revival of the blood libel myth (the latest incident of note occurred in 1928 in New York, wherein "a state trooper questioned the rabbi and asked him whether Jews offered human sacrifices or used blood in rituals"[3]).

However, more commonly, in the weeks leading up to Passover, rabbis such as myself receive the sadly predictable emails and calls from Christians and Messianics asking if they can join in or host their own Seders in order to "re-create the Passover like Jesus celebrated." We will discuss Messianics and other non-Jewish sects, such as Jews for Jesus, in a later chapter. Focusing on Christians, however, we rabbis (and Jews alike) see countless invitations around Passover on Twitter and other social media platforms to Seders. One such invitation from Harvest Time Church states, "COME TO [*sic*] a special online Passover Seder. Christians can discover their Jewish roots, Jewish people can discover the Passover's fulfillment, and God's love can melt all our hearts!"

Situations like this blur the line between what is appropriate and what is appropriative. As stated above, the Passover Seder was created rabbinically after the fall of the Second Temple in 70 CE. The most important point to take from this for Christians is that Jesus never celebrated the Passover Seder, as the Seder had yet to be invented. This is an important learning moment for our Christian friends, clergy and laypeople alike. Nevertheless, Christians within the United States and elsewhere each year attempt to morph the Jewish ritual of the Passover Seder into their own, such as the following example in which Judaism has been completely lost altogether with regard to Passover:

> Shepherd's Chapel of Gravette held their annual Passover Meeting . . . in Springdale, AR. Passover is a Christian religious holiday commemorating the sacrifice Jesus made for the world and celebrating His resurrection. . . . 252 of those attending were baptized.[4]

While this discovery may bring a bit of humor to the situation, it is truly upsetting to Jews to see a Jewish ritual, one that did not exist during the time of Jesus, being appropriated, changed, and rewritten into a new (and false) narrative.

Once, when I was a student at university, around Passover time, I was walking down Commonwealth Avenue on my way to class and found myself face-to-face with a Christian presentation on the street. The young men and women were drawing art on a canvas. On one side of the canvas was a painting of the blood on the doorposts of the Israelite homes as the angel of death passed over the houses; on the other side was the blood dripping from Jesus's cross. At the time, I was uneducated about the substantial amount of "church Seders" and appropriation that occurred (and occurs) in many Christian denominations, wherein Judaism is appropriated and replaced with ideas such as the death of the firstborn foreshadows the death of Jesus; the lamb without blemish parallels Jesus, the Lamb of God; the lamb's blood on wooden doorposts of Israelite homes anticipates Jesus's blood on the wooden cross; the three pieces of matzah represent the Trinity; and the broken middle matzah constitutes the body of Jesus (the middle member of the Trinity) broken on the cross.[5]

Christian theologians such as Joel Marcus of Duke University Divinity School work hard in their attempt to find similarities between the Last Supper and the Passover Seder. Marcus, for instance, calls attention to the so-called *ha lachma* (Aramaic for "This is the bread"), a brief passage traditionally recited at the opening of the Seder—"This is the bread of affliction that our ancestors ate in Egypt"[6]—and compares it to the words of institution, the words Christians use to bless the bread in communion, where Jesus says, "Take, eat, this is my body broken for you."[7]

This practice of viewing the "seder through the prism of Christian theology" is an act that diminishes the Jewish ritual of Passover and rewrites a new historical narrative, removing completely the original meaning of the Seder and the holiday surrounding it.[8] While a majority of Christians may be acting out of good faith and do not intend maliciousness appropriation, they are participating in, whether they see it or not, the practice of replacement theology. The term *replacement theology*, or *supersessionism*, is described by both Jewish and Christian theologians. For example, Christian theologian R. Kendall Soulen notes three categories of supersessionism—punitive, economic, and structural—identified by Christian theologians:[9]

> *Punitive supersessionism* is represented by such Christian thinkers as Hippolytus of Rome, Origin, and Martin Luther. It is the view that Jews who reject Jesus as the Jewish Messiah are consequently condemned by God, forfeiting the promises due to them in the covenants.
>
> *Economic supersessionism* is used in the technical theological sense of function. It is the view that the practical purpose of the nation of Israel in God's plan is replaced by the role of the church. It is represented by writers such as Justin Martyr, Augustine, and Barth.
>
> *Structural supersessionism* is Soulen's term for the de facto marginalization of the Old Testament (Hebrew Scriptures) as normative for Christian thought: "Structural supersessionism . . . renders the Hebrew Scriptures largely indecisive for shaping Christian convictions about how God works as Consummator and Redeemer to engage humankind in universal and enduring ways."[10]

One can then easily see why Jews would be offended by replacement theology and Christian supersessionist theology. Even if not intended as malicious, comparing the Passover Seder to the sacrifice of Christ or even the sacrament of communion can be viewed by Jews as a form of replacement. Situations in which maliciousness is intended, such as when missionaries make it a point to use the Christian Seder to attract Jews and convert them through subterfuge, deserve a different response.

But for those Christians who are misinformed and genuinely wish to strengthen their own religion by learning from its predecessor, learning moments between Jews and Christians can be productive and fruitful exercises.

Years ago, at my congregation on a Saturday morning, a teenage Christian girl came to our Shabbat (Sabbath) services to learn about Jewish worship. When the Torah, our holiest text, was passed around the congregation and came to her during what is known as the ritual of *hakafah*, the Christian girl touched it and then, in an instance of pure beauty, crossed herself, fusing Judaism and Christianity, which for her came together for the first time in a very real way. While some of the older Jewish congregants sneered at the act, I quickly came to the girl's defense, saying to our congregation, "Could there be any more amazing thing to see than a young Christian person's faith reenergized by learning the Jewish roots and connection, a moment when Judaism serves as the teacher and helper to Christianity through peace and education rather than tension and violence?" I retell this story because the Passover Seder can be viewed the same way, as the same opportunity for those who wish to learn and bring about a deeper understanding of their faith. Just as the young Christian girl in my pews had to be educated as to what the Torah represented, so too do the Christian guests at our Seder tables need to be educated as to why Passover is a purely Jewish ritual, not a Christian one, but a ritual nonetheless that can inspire them.

Christians are traditionally taught through interpretation of the Synoptic Gospels (Mark, Matthew, and Luke) that the "Last Supper" was a Passover Seder. They come to this conclusion primarily because of the misunderstanding of the Gospel of Mark's identification of the Last Supper as a "Passover meal":

On the first day of the Festival of Unleavened Bread, when it was customary to sacrifice the Passover lamb, Jesus' disciples asked him, "Where do you want us to go and make preparations for you to eat the Passover?"[11]

Herein is where the confusion begins, as modern Christians associate the words "Passover" and "Festival of Unleavened Bread" with the Passover Seder. However, a historical understanding of the verse provides a clearer view. The Feast of Unleavened Bread and the Pascal (Passover) sacrifice were both known to Israelite culture and celebrated during Jesus's time in the first century CE. Their origins are seen in the Torah, as stated in Exodus 12:17–18 (brackets in the original):

> You shall observe the [Feast of] Unleavened Bread, for on this very day I brought your ranks out of the land of Egypt; you shall observe this day throughout the ages as an institution for all time. In the first month, from the fourteenth day of the month at evening, you shall eat unleavened bread until the twenty-first day of the month at evening.

The Torah also states that there was a Passover sacrifice, the slaughter on the eve of the Feast of Unleavened Bread:

> The LORD spoke to Moses in the wilderness of Sinai, on the first new moon of the second year following the exodus from the land of Egypt, saying: Let the Israelite people offer the passover sacrifice at its set time: you shall offer it on the fourteenth day of this month, at twilight, at its set time; you shall offer it in accordance with all its rules and rites.[12]

As Robert Alter and other biblical scholars note, it is most plausible that the Feast of Unleavened Bread and the Passover sacrifice "were originally two different holidays—*matsot* (agricultural) and *pesah* (pastoral)—that were drawn together in the literary formulation" of the Torah text.[13] In other words, two first-century celebrations—that is, the Feast of Unleavened Bread and the Passover sacrifice—did exist during Jesus's time, but at that time, they did not constitute the Passover Seder. Scholars are helpful in pointing out that at the Last Supper, as told by the Gospels, there is no mention of matzah, unleavened bread (instead, bread is mentioned), nor is there any mention of bitter herbs or of the exodus from Egypt.[14] Indeed, the Passover Seder had yet to be created because the Seder itself was a replacement of the ritual of the slaughtering of the Passover sacrifice, which only could be done when the temple stood. When the temple was destroyed in 70 CE, a rabbinic replacement needed to be found to stand in for the previous sacrificial ritual. As we know, the Gospel writers had their agendas when attempting to retell the story of the events leading up to the Passion Narrative. By adding the description of the Passover ritual to the story, the author of the Gospel of Mark "tried to transform an ordinary Last Supper meal into Passover observance so that he could correlate Passover, the festival of physical and political freedom for the Jews, with Jesus' death, which brought spiritual freedom for humanity."[15]

As we will discuss more in chapter 5, the above practice was common for the Gospel authors—namely, to connect Jewish festivals and rituals to Jesus in order to form a bond with the Hebrew Bible and Jewish practice. However, scholarship and history tell us not only that the Passover Seder originated after Jesus's time but that neither Jesus the Jew nor pre–70 CE Christians ever practiced a Seder of any kind, let alone celebrations like those that many churches today stage to "reenact" the Last Supper:

> The synoptic account stretches credulity, not just because it depicts something unlikely, but because it fails to recognize the

unlikely and problematic nature of what it depicts. It is almost as if the synoptic tradition has lost all familiarity with contemporary Jewish practice. And if they have lost familiarity with that, they have probably lost familiarity with reliable historical information as well.[16]

While biblical and archaeological scholars attempt to understand exactly how a first-century CE Jew would have commemorated the Passover sacrifice and the Feast of Unleavened Bread, one thing is clear: it was not a modern-day Passover Seder. This is the most important distinction in this section, in that by Christians co-opting the later symbolic rituals of the rabbinic Passover Seder, they do nothing to honor the historical Jesus or the rites he may have practiced. Instead, by doing so, Christians only purloin a beloved and sacred Jewish ritual in a misguided attempt to place Jesus imagery into a ritual of which he knew nothing.[17]

Hanukkah

Passover is not the only holiday that is appropriated (or misappropriated) by Christians. One need only skim social media in the late winter to see the all too familiar flurry of posts by Christians, including posting Hanukkah menorahs with Christian messages, adding "Yeshua" and other messianic themes to Hanukkah items, and posting articles about why Christians should also celebrate the Festival of Lights. Again, Hanukkah need not be appropriated by Christians, as it is a story that occurred well before Jesus's time.

To begin with the basics, the story of Hanukkah (translated as "dedication" and known commonly as the Festival of Lights) comes from two distinct sources in Jewish Scripture. The first is from the first and second books of Maccabees, apocryphal texts that do not appear in the Jewish canon but do appear in many Christian canons (more on that in the next chapter). The first two books of Maccabees record the story of Judah Maccabee and his family as they fought against the forced Hellenization of Jews and won liberation from the Seleucid Empire. The text states, "The Maccabees were fighters from a priestly Jewish family who successfully waged war against the Seleucids and rededicated the Second Temple in Jerusalem—which is now commemorated on Hanukkah. The Maccabees established the Hasmonean dynasty, which ruled from 167 BCE to 37 BCE."[18]

However, most Jews do not use these apocryphal texts to retell the story of the Maccabees for religious purposes. Rather, Jewish ritual was formed around the story of the "Hanukkah miracle," the mystical story of the miracle of the oil that is found in the Talmud, tractate Shabbat 21b:10, written nearly six hundred years after the time of the Maccabees:

> The Gemara asks: What is Hanukkah? The Gemara answers: The Sages taught in *Megillat Ta'anit*: On the twenty-fifth of Kislev, the days of Hanukkah are eight. One may not eulogize on them and one may not fast on them. What is the reason? When the Greeks entered the Sanctuary they defiled all the oils that were in the Sanctuary by touching them. And when the Hasmonean monarchy overcame them and emerged victorious over them, they searched and found only one cruse of oil that was placed with the seal of the High Priest, undisturbed by the Greeks. And there was sufficient oil there to light the candelabrum for only one day. A miracle occurred and they lit the candelabrum from it eight days. The next year the Sages instituted those days and made them holidays with recitation of *hallel* and special thanksgiving in prayer and blessings.

This story, which is a rabbinical creation, was inserted into the historical narrative to add a theological angle on what was a relatively secular portrait of the defeat of a tyrannical empire. The story as told below contains the narrative of worshipping God and cultic rituals but leaves out God's direct involvement in the purification of the temple and the conquering of enemies:

> Now on the five and twentieth day of the ninth month, which is called the month Casleu, in the hundred forty and eighth year, they rose up betimes in the morning, And offered sacrifice according to the law upon the new altar of burnt offerings, which they had made. Look, at what time and what day the heathen had profaned it, even in that was it dedicated with songs, and cithers, and harps, and cymbals. Then all the people fell upon their faces, worshipping and praising the God of heaven, who had given them good success. And so they kept the dedication of the altar eight days and offered burnt offerings with gladness, and sacrificed the sacrifice of deliverance and praise. . . . Moreover Judas and his brethren with the whole congregation of Israel ordained, that the days of the dedication of the altar should be kept in their season from year to year by the space of eight days, from the five and twentieth day of the month Kislev with mirth and gladness.[19]

The fact that the Hanukkah story of the "miracle" is a rabbinic creation from half a millennium later, admittedly, comes as a shock to most Jews who have always thought it was recorded in historical accounts. However, there is holiness and importance in understanding that "the Talmudic story of the miraculous oil was chosen by the rabbis as the 'official' etiology of the festival of Hanukkah because they wanted a narrative that would function as part of a long tradition of narratives involving the recovery of a lost or hidden object from a bygone era."[20]

So when we see Christians looking to "celebrate Hanukkah as Jesus did" by, for example, lighting the Hanukkah menorah—as seen by scholars such as Jerry R. Lancaster and R. Larry Overstreet, who "argue that the healing of the blind man in John 9 shows the light of the world shining on the spiritually blind akin to the lamps of Hanukkah"[21]—or focusing on the Shamash (the "servant" candle that lights the other candles on the menorah to represent "the sacred flesh of the Son of God bearing its flame of divinity. He hears the Word of God saying of Himself, 'I am the light of the world'"),[22] there is an inherent disconnect that must be addressed.

These references clearly are linked to the historical story of the Maccabees told in the apocryphal writings and not linked to the rabbinic tale told in the Talmud. The disconnect is that Christians are not observing the true Jewish Hanukkah celebration. It is also important to remind Christians that Jesus did not "celebrate" Hanukkah as we do today, because the celebration was not invented until long after his time. How Hanukkah was observed by first-century Jews would not include lighting the Hanukkah menorah, or eating latkes, or discussing the great miracle that occurred, since those theological elements were added by the Talmudic sages later, as they felt the Hanukkah story lacked theological elements.

Also important to remember is that the Talmud, which held that the Hanukkah celebration was deemed "anti-Christian," was burned by Christians, such as in Paris in the thirteenth century under the authority of Pope Gregory IX, the inquisitions of the fifteenth and sixteenth centuries, and even eighteenth-century Poland under the guise of Bishop Nicholas Dembowski.[23] Why, then, would Christians, who have rejected the text, seek to embrace a story and the celebration that came from it?

Ironically, the story of Hanukkah is that of a religious group fighting against forced assimilation by another majority culture.

In other words, parallels could easily be made between the Has-
moneans under Hellenistic rule and Jews living in a Christian
majority country, such as the United States. During the winter
season, in America and elsewhere, Christmas is visible everywhere, with lights, trees, wreaths, nativity scenes, and the like
on every street corner and Christmas music in every store. The
unfortunate side effect of blending Jewish and Christian holiday
cultures can be seen in the sales of Hanukkah nativity scenes,
Hanukkah Christmas ornaments, and Magen David Christmas
tree toppers. More to the point of our discussion, the story of
the rebellion against the Seleucids and the victory of the Has-
moneans has nothing to do with Jesus, Christmas, or prophets
but rather is one of many stories within Jewish history of Jews
fighting off those who would seek to convert them. Unfortunately, this irony is lost upon many Christians, especially those
who are no strangers to proselytization or seeking to convert
Jews, who wish to take the side of the Maccabees.

Christians should tread carefully when looking to become
involved in the process of appropriating historical Judaism.
Again, this is not to deter Christians who wish, with pure intentions, to learn more about the Jewish foundations of Christianity and experience Jewish rituals in their original form, without
inserting Christian views. They are welcome guests as we light
menorahs, eat latkes, and spin dreidels. But they must take the
lead in educating one another, creating boundaries around what
is and is not appropriate in regard to intruding Jewish holidays.
It has always been my policy to kindly ask Christians to leave
Hanukkah be and joyfully celebrate their own holiday of Christmas during the winter months. After all, there's plenty of pres-
ents and food to go around.[24]

Shavuot/Pentecost

Shavuot (weeks) is an easily googleable Jewish holiday. Its origin comes from one of the ancient three agricultural festivals mentioned in the Torah: "Shavuot was called the festival of the wheat harvest, *Hag Hakatzir* (Exod 23:16) or a day for bringing first-fruits to the Temple, *Yom Habikurim* (Num 28:26), but not *Zman Matan Toratenu*, the time of giving of the Law."[25] The passages in the Torah that speak about the "first fruits" are as follows.

Exodus, for instance, reads,

> Three times a year you shall hold a festival for Me: You shall observe the Feast of Unleavened Bread—eating unleavened bread for seven days as I have commanded you—at the set time in the month of Abib, for in it you went forth from Egypt; and none shall appear before Me empty-handed; and the Feast of the Harvest, of the first fruits of your work, of what you sow in the field; and the Feast of Ingathering at the end of the year, when you gather in the results of your work from the field.[26]

And Numbers reads,

> On the day of the first fruits, your Feast of Weeks, when you bring an offering of new grain to the LORD, you shall observe a sacred occasion: you shall not work at your occupations.[27]

These verses were then interpreted by the sages of the second to the fifth century from the Mishnah and midrash. For example, Mishnah Bikkurim 3 says,

> How does one set aside bikkurim? A man goes down into his field, he sees a fig that ripened, or a cluster of grapes that

ripened, or a pomegranate that ripened, he ties a reed-rope around it and says: "Let these be bikkurim." Rabbi Shimon says: even so, he must again designate them as bikkurim after they have been plucked from the soil.[28]

However, like many of the agricultural beginnings of Jewish holidays, those of Shavuot were transformed into something far more theological. The rabbis after the second century took the meaning of Shavuot to a whole new level, eventually linking the "weeks" in between Passover and the festival to represent the days the Israelites spent at the base of Mount Sinai, when the Israelites experienced the communal revelation of the receiving of the Torah:

After the Temple was destroyed and the Israelites could no longer bring the first fruits of their harvest as offerings, Talmudic rabbis reframed the holiday. The Rabbis ascribed Shavuot to the biblical story which recounts how, after the Exodus from Egypt, the Israelites proceeded to Mount Sinai in the desert. Moses ascended the mountain to meet God, who gave him the Ten Commandments, which were written on two tablets to be delivered to the Israelites.[29]

While the details of this transition are relatively unknown, we know that the rabbis sought to bring an agricultural and cultic holiday into the era after the temple was destroyed: "The reframing of Shavuot is an example of how the nation's leaders sought to mold a society that could survive in exile. In our day, our leaders are faced with the same problem in reverse: how to build a Jewish society that can hold together as a free people in our own land."[30]

No matter the controversy or reason behind the transition, Shavuot is now a holiday that Jews celebrate in the weeks after

Passover to commemorate the giving of the Torah at Sinai. Shavuot is celebrated with sweet treats as well as a night of studying. This is vastly different from the Christian version of what is known as Pentecost. Logistically, the celebration happens around the same time as Shavuot. *Pentecost* is the Greek translation of "fiftieth," since it occurs fifty days from Easter; Shavuot is celebrated on the fiftieth day after Passover. But the true meaning behind the Jewish holiday is unknown to most Christians, who view Pentecost through the lens of the New Testament book of Acts, chapter 2:

> When the day of Pentecost came, they were all together in one place. Suddenly a sound like the blowing of a violent wind came from heaven and filled the whole house where they were sitting. They saw what seemed to be tongues of fire that separated and came to rest on each of them. All of them were filled with the Holy Spirit and began to speak in other tongues as the Spirit enabled them.[31]

Some refer to this event as the birth of the Christian movement, as the apostles of Jesus received the Holy Spirit and began to speak in tongues and proclaim the gospel.

At this point in the historic time line of Judaism, Shavuot had yet to be transformed from the agricultural festival to the commemoration of the giving of the Torah, but more importantly, for followers of Jesus, Pentecost ceased being connected to the Jewish holiday and became a fully new celebration through Christian eyes. In fact, when one googles *Pentecost*, it lists the definition (quite rightly) as a "Christian holiday." Therefore, while Jews celebrate Shavuot at the same (or similar) time as Christians celebrate Pentecost, at this point, millennia later, the two holidays have virtually nothing in common. Both sprung from the same seed of the agricultural festival prescribed in the

Torah, but they became two very different plants. While Christians may wish to celebrate Shavuot with Jews (to which they are welcome), it would be to celebrate the giving of the Torah at Sinai and that revelation rather than the Christian one involving the Holy Spirit, which does not exist in Jewish theology.

A Word about Other Holidays

Besides Passover and Hanukkah, which are the Jewish holidays that occur adjacent to the Christian holidays of Easter and Christmas, respectively, there are other (and more important in some cases) holidays that occur during the Jewish calendar that call for Christian awareness and sensitivity. What's most important is that Christians respect Jewish traditions when interested in sharing these holidays. For example, Sukkoth, known also as the Feast of Tabernacles, is familiar to Christians, as it is mentioned in the Gospel of John, chapter 7:

> After this, Jesus went around in Galilee. He did not want to go about in Judea because the Jewish leaders there were looking for a way to kill him. But when the Jewish Festival of Tabernacles was near, Jesus' brothers said to him, "Leave Galilee and go to Judea, so that your disciples there may see the works you do. No one who wants to become a public figure acts in secret. Since you are doing these things, show yourself to the world." For even his own brothers did not believe in him.[32]

While it may be difficult for Christians reading the Gospel of John to separate the Feast of Tabernacles from the accusations of "the Jews," the holiday of Sukkoth is one to be shared with Jews and Christians alike as a time of welcoming and understanding. It would be a pleasure for Jews to host Christians who wish to experience a Sukkoth service or celebration so they can experience perhaps something close to what Jesus celebrated in the first century. Though, as we have discussed above, Christians should keep in mind that Jewish rituals and holiday celebrations have evolved significantly since the first century CE.

For other holidays, such as Shabbat, Rosh Hashanah, Yom Kippur, Simchat Torah, Tisha B'Av, or Tu B'Shvat, Christians are always welcome as guests to sit in and experience them with us. I highly recommend that those who wish to learn about Judaism and Jewish holidays reach out to rabbis in the area so they are directed to the correct sources, since the internet can be a problematic place to find accuracy. Nevertheless, it brings Jews great joy to educate Christians about and share with them Jewish heritage, especially for a reason that many Christians may overlook.

For millennia, Jews have lived under the rule, either directly or indirectly, of Christians, experiencing ghettoization, persecution, restrictions in law, pogroms, torture, forced conversion, genocide, or simply a Christian majority country that structures its daily life around Christian beliefs. When Christians come to learn with Jews about holidays or any other topic, it provides an opportunity for Jews to remove the stereotypes and form new images of themselves in the eyes of Christians. They can demonstrate a deeper understanding of their faith that goes beyond the picture drawn in the Gospels, and they can build bridges of understanding that can lead to the demolition of supersessionism or anti-Semitism. Many Christian laypeople may not be fully aware of the occurrences in antiquity, medieval times, or even modern time periods in which Jews suffered directly or indirectly under the hands of Christian authority. The celebration of Jewish holidays is a perfect opportunity to break that cycle and begin a dialogue of equality, with no agenda to convert or condemn. A rabbi of the early twentieth century, Ferdinand M. Isserman of St. Louis, Missouri, once wrote in one of his many sermons on the topic,

> What is true of all humanity is true especially of the relations between Jews and between Christians. The difficulties which have existed between them in the past and which exist between them today are based almost entirely on those suspicions and fears which are the children of ignorance. Show me the Christian who knows the Jew and Judaism and I will show you the Christian in whose heart there dwells no prejudice. Show me the Jew who knows the Christian and Christianity and I will show you the Jew who is appreciative of Christians and of their faith.[33]

Rabbi Isserman's words, almost a century old, resonate with Jews today because they strike at the heart of the matter in our world. If hate is the child of ignorance, then peace must be the child of education. Far too often, we find ourselves without opportunity for genuine, raw dialogue between Christians and Jews. There simply are not enough face-to-face, difficult though respectful encounters with one another. And yet it is within *these* encounters that stereotypes wash away, and we learn that what distinguishes Judaism from Christianity need not separate us, and fundamentalism and fanaticism can find no ground upon which to stand.[34]

I urge Christians to reach out to synagogues and rabbis to experience Jewish holidays with no agenda except education. Christians are always welcome, but they should be understanding and thoughtful about the weariness Jews may feel toward them. It is up to those members of Christianity to break down the walls of fear, express no desire for conversion or subterfuge, and simply speak to Jews as equals or, better yet, as teachers to help them better understand the Christian theological views of the Messiah.

Judeo-Christian Values

Tucked beneath the subject of holidays is the long-debated topic of "Judeo-Christian values." While this subject could be put in many different parts of this book, I felt it important to put it here, as the subject of holidays is a confusing intersection between Jews and Christians, and this term, *Judeo-Christian*, is where much is lost. Distinct lines between Jewish and Christian celebrations of holidays do exist, but there are similarities and common themes that we can rally around to bring about better interfaith understanding and dialogue.

However, this leads to a larger discussion of the common expression that the United States was and is based on Judeo-Christian values.[35] This understanding is simply not accurate. America was not founded on a Judeo-Christian value system. James Loeffler, Jay Berkowitz Professor of Jewish History at the University of Virginia, says it this way:

> The "Judeo-Christian tradition" was one of 20th-century America's greatest political inventions. An ecumenical marketing meme for combatting godless communism, the catchphrase long did the work of animating American conservatives in the Cold War battle. For a brief time, canny liberals also embraced the phrase as a rhetorical pathway of inclusion into postwar American democracy for Jews, Catholics, and Black Americans. In a world divided by totalitarianism abroad and racial segregation at home, the notion of a shared American religious heritage promised racial healing and national unity.[36]

This is similar to the addition of "under God" to the Pledge of Allegiance in the mid-twentieth century. Most people assume the revised version is the original. More recently, the term *Judeo-Christian* has been used specifically as an exclusionary device against other religions—"most often used to draw a line between imagined Christian values and a perceived (but false) threat of Muslim immigration," as a colleague of mine explains so succinctly.[37] "Judeo-Christian" isn't a thing. It (a) positions Jews and Christians against Muslims, is Islamophobic; (b) elides the Christian oppression and murder of Jews over more than a thousand years; and (c) ignores Jewish civilization worldwide and facts of key Jewish developments in the Middle East and North Africa.[38]

Indeed, the term *Judeo-Christian* has been used to isolate and discriminate against Islam, while those supporting the term seem to forget that "Jews have been systematically excluded from and terrorized by states that claim this Judeo-Christian foundation."[39] Unfortunately, the term, misguided as it is, has become a "dog whistle" used by the religious right: "The phrase appears with regularity in rhetorical attacks on Islam and the progressive left, in attempts to restrict immigration and LGBTQ rights, and in arguments in favor of religious freedom that would collapse the wall of separation between Church and state."[40]

In other words, this term (originally "a word for Jewish converts to Christianity"[41]) has been weaponized to discriminate against those of Muslim origin as well as any other minorities who don't fit a particular interpretation of the Bible. This argument came up in the past few years when "biblical literacy" bills were sponsored by right-winged politicians attempting to have the Bible taught in public schools. Just as the term *Judeo-Christian* is a loaded one with hidden agendas, so is the idea of teaching the Bible in schools:

Hebrew and Greek, as stated above, contain many ambiguities, but translators do not. Rather, they frequently push their subconscious or conscious agendas on the reader by choosing meanings of words that fit their theologies. . . . Jews, Muslims, Atheists, Hindus, Buddhists, Bahai, and many others would be subjected to a very particular "Bible literacy," meaning a Christian interpretation of the words of the Bible by Christian translators, with Christian theology packed into the choices of the words on the pages.[42]

It was clear immediately—to Jews, at least—that teaching the Bible in public schools meant teaching Christianity in schools, just as it is clear that those politicians who weaponize the word *Judeo-Christian* mean, simply, Christian values. The truth of the matter, ironically, is that "Christianity" is exactly what "Judeo-Christian" means, but not for the reason the politicians would like. Despite the long history of prejudiced, anti-communistic, and minority-suppressing uses of the term, no such thing as "Judeo-Christian" values exists.

To put it simply, Judaism and Christianity began to evolve completely differently in the second and third centuries CE. As we discussed in previous chapters, cultic and biblical Judaism changed dramatically when the Second Temple was destroyed and began to transform under the guidance of the rabbis and based on documents such as the Mishnah, Talmud, and midrash. The followers of Jesus wrote the texts of the New Testament, and the Christian church authorized a canon of Scripture over the first four centuries CE. That means that Jews and Christians have been on separate paths for over 1,900 years.

So what does this mean? Quite simply, the values inside biblical Judaism were (and are) interpreted through a Jewish lens by the rabbis, through the books of law and interpretation, and finally into law codes and responsa that now form modern Judaism. Parallel to this were the values that Christians gleaned from biblical Judaism, which focused on theological ideas, including the typological predictions of the Messiah (Jesus) and reinterpreting the laws and stories of the "Old Testament" through the lens of a "new" one. In other words, there never were any Jewish-Christian values, nor can there ever be because as soon as the Jesus movement began in the first century CE, the followers of Jesus began to rework and reinterpret Jewish values into their own.

Let us understand this idea further through a commandment that has come to be known as the Golden Rule. When interpreting the Levitical commandment "Love your neighbor," Jesus, according to the Gospel of Matthew, states, "So in everything, do to others what you would have them do to you, for this sums up the Law and the Prophets."[43] We are right to assume that Jesus most likely was aware of the Jewish teachings of his time and before, including the words of the famous rabbi Hillel, who, when challenged a generation earlier by a gentile to summarize the Torah while the gentile stood on one foot, stated, "What is hateful to you, do not do to your fellow, that is the whole Torah; the rest is the explanation, go and learn it."[44] These words are recorded in the Mishnah, a rabbinic text of collected teachings dating from the first century BCE to the second century CE. It is not surprising, then, that the Gospel writers, being aware of the literature of their day, were moved by Hillel's words and sought to restate them in the form of the affirmative through Jesus's voice.[45] While this can be taken as a wonderful example of a similarity between Judaism and Christianity, one that I personally have used to build bridges of dialogue, the contexts in which these sayings arose are different. In the Gospel of Matthew, the context is as follows:

Which of you, if your son asks for bread, will give him a stone? Or if he asks for a fish, will give him a snake? If you, then, though you are evil, know how to give good gifts to your children, how much more will your Father in heaven give good gifts to those who ask him! So in everything, do to others what you would have them do to you, for this sums up the Law and the Prophets.[46]

The context for Hillel that occurs in the Talmud, Tractate Shabbat 31a is this:

Another time a non-Jew came before Shammai and said, "I will convert if you can teach me the entire Torah while I stand on one foot." Shammai pushed the non-Jews aside with the ruler that was in his hand. The non-Jew came before Hillel and Hillel converted him saying, "What is hateful to you, do not do to your neighbor, that is the entire Torah, the rest is just commentary, now go and study."

The Gospel of Matthew mentions "Father in heaven," which is in accordance with very Christian ideals and theology. The Talmud tells of a story of a proselyte, one who wished to convert to Judaism, and how to lead those down the path of conversion (at least according to two sages, Hillel and Shammai). While both teachers, Hillel and Jesus, spoke nearly the same words, they were said for very different reasons and within different contexts. Context is at the heart of the discrepancies between Judeo-Christian values. Often, Jews and Christians see passages in the Hebrew Bible / Old Testament in different contexts and times. The placement of teachings, the audience intended, and the theologies embedded cannot and should not be ignored. In other words, values may seem similar on the surface but underneath are quite different and have different purposes.

I bring this to the attention of the reader not only for a lesson in political misuse of religious terminology but as a blanket to spread over the beginnings of dialogue between Jews and Christians. If there ever was a term in antiquity entitled *Judeo-Christianity*, it would be described this way, as Daniel Boyarin summarizes:

> Judaeo-Christianity, not now Jewish Christianity, but the entire multiform cultural system, should be seen as the original cauldron of contentious, dissonant, sometimes friendly, more frequently hostile, fecund religious productivity out of which ultimately precipitated two institutions at the end of late antiquity: orthodox Christianity and rabbinic Judaism.[47]

To return to the original topic from above, when Jews and Christians approach each other's holidays, the latter cannot simply say to the former, "We want to celebrate what Jesus celebrated." Not only is that statement historically inaccurate, as rabbinic Judaism changed many, if not all, of the holidays that modern Jews celebrate today, but the reason for holidays in the Jewish tradition and the values associated with them have been co-opted by certain Christian thought and evolution so that when some Christians attempt to celebrate Jewish holidays (without Jewish supervision), the original value system is lost. In sum, Judeo-Christian values do not exist, but there are similarities between Jewish values and Christian values.

Key Takeaways from Chapter 3

1. Jesus's Last Supper was not a Passover Seder. This revelation for Christians should encourage them to not attempt to create "Christian Seders," as the practice did not exist during Jesus's time. Moreover, they should avoid replacement theology and appropriation in terms of the Passover

Seder. That being said, they are welcome to attend Jewish Passover Seders for educational and interfaith purposes.

2. The story of Hanukkah comes from both the first two books of Maccabees and the teachings in the Talmud. The former occurred centuries before Jesus was born, and the latter, centuries after he died. The story of Hanukkah is about Jews overcoming a Hellenistic oppressive force that wished to convert them. It is inappropriate for Christians to insert themselves into this story. They, however, are welcome to join Jews in commemorating this holiday but should avoid doing so on their own.

3. Jewish holidays are perfect opportunities for Christians to engage in important interfaith dialogue and understanding. With so much resentment and fear on the side of the Jews, based on the violent history under Christian rule and influence, Christians should use these holidays as occasions to mend broken fences and build bridges of care and appreciation.

4. *Judeo-Christian* is a term that should be removed from both Jewish and Christian conversations, as it not only finds its origins as weaponized prejudice against non-Christians but also muddies the waters in the distinct differences between how Jews and how Christians see the world and their own teachings.

4

THE DIFFERENCE
IN OUR CANONS

As a rabbi and a biblical scholar, I end up raining on a lot of people's parades—whether it is telling my congregation that the Hanukkah "miracle" was a rabbinic invention and probably didn't happen or telling adult learners that there is no archaeological evidence that Israelites were ever slaves in Egypt. Another surprising "aha" moment has to do with a phrase that is common to both Jewish and Christian experiences: "The Hebrew Bible and the Old Testament are the same thing." Unfortunately, this is not the case, and this chapter will discuss, among other topics, why the Hebrew Bible and the Old Testament are very much *not* the same book.

Building the Hebrew Bible

While some observant and fundamentalist Jews and Christians alike view the biblical time line as a historical chronology that begins with the deity transmitting the holy writings to humanity, the picture is much more complicated. In a world where we have access to science, literary analysis, and archaeological evidence (or a lack thereof), we can no longer afford to embrace that "flat-earther" view. To ignore the discoveries of science, biblical analysis, and newly found evidence would be the equivalent of putting our heads in the sand. One need only look at the Mesopotamian, Egyptian, Babylonian, Canaanite, and Ugaritic writings to see that much of the Torah comes from a reworking of Near Eastern texts that far predate the books we know. Indeed, the myths of Enūma Eliš with the Genesis creation story, the epics of Atrahasis or Gilgamesh with the flood of Noah, the Hammurabi Code with laws in Exodus are just some examples that appear to have influenced the messages of the biblical authors. They transformed the legends of their neighboring civilizations into their own. Like the works that came before it, the Torah should be seen as a collection of ancient myths or beliefs, with stories representing allegories and metaphors. This is important yet difficult to understand when considering the creation and canonization of the Hebrew Bible.

Gary Rendsburg, for example, the chair of the Jewish history department at Rutgers University, makes his views about historicity clear in his piece called "Israel without the Bible."[1] In the article, Rendsburg declares himself a "maximalist" as opposed to a "minimalist" with regard to biblical interpretation. The former, according to Rendsburg, believes that "the Bible reflects true history until it can be proved otherwise," and the latter assumes "the Bible is literary fiction, until it can be proved otherwise."[2] He is explicit in his support of the maximalist view and just as explicit in his criticism of the minimalist view. Rendsburg's education, résumé, and authorship are all impressive and include archaeological undertakings and a strong research background. Yet this does not explain his virulent chastising of biblical scholarship, which, no doubt, many of his colleagues hold dear. In my opinion, the maximalist view is not as productive or fruitful a method as minimalist biblical criticism.

The minimalist view, what also may be called the historical-critical method, is crucial in helping us discover how biblical books came into existence in their present forms. Alexander

Fantalkin and Oren Tal concur, saying, "The canonization of the Pentateuch has preoccupied scholars from different disciplines from antiquity to the present. However, two major questions still require an explanation: when did it happen and why did it happen?"[3] The Torah, let alone the Bible, was not written from beginning to end in a smooth chronological line. Rather, books of the Torah were shaped and added to piece by piece and most likely were not set in stone without redaction until the time of Jesus's birth. Scholars have been able to theorize and conclude that some parts of the Torah were written in a postexilic time, after the destruction of the Great Temple in 587 BCE. In fact, "these post-exilic attempts to organize sets of biblical books into subcollections suggest some religious consensus regarding their meaning and shed light on the ensuing biblical interpretation."[4] What existed for centuries were books in their original formats, in what scholars call the "proto-Torah." If you pick a time within the thousand years before the first century CE, you could read, certainly, parts of the stories we have come to know in fragments of proto-Genesis, proto-Leviticus, and the like. It was not until much later that certain authorities had the power to add and remove particular aspects, tie stories together with an ideological overlay, and edit and redact them in order to shape the books so that they told the stories in ways that supported their ideology.

An example of this is seen in the work of biblical scholars such as Martin Noth and Philip R. Davies, who theorize that the book of Deuteronomy was itself a late addition to the canon that perhaps originally connected the book of Numbers with the book of Joshua. Davies argues, "Hence the account of the death of Moses . . . originally stood at the end of Numbers. Numbers 36:13 was composed to introduce Deuteronomy, which was detached from Joshua to Kings by means of the additional final chapters, leaving the rest of the 'Deuteronomic History' to move into the orbit of a different canon."[5]

When reading the end of Numbers, verse 36:13 does stand out as perhaps an insert added later:

> The daughters of Zelophehad did as the LORD had commanded Moses: Mahlah, Tirzah, Hoglah, Milcah, and Noah, Zelophehad's daughters, were married to sons of their uncles, marrying into clans of descendants of Manasseh son of Joseph; and so their share remained in the tribe of their father's clan. These are the commandments and regulations that the LORD enjoined upon the Israelites, through Moses, on the steppes of Moab, at the Jordan near Jericho.[6]

Further, Davies and Noth argue that at the end of Numbers 26 until Numbers 27:23, it certainly seems like things are wrapping up for Moses and that perhaps his death was originally planned for this spot:

> Moses spoke to the LORD, saying, "Let the LORD, Source of the breath of all flesh, appoint someone over the community who shall go out before them and come in before them, and who shall take them out and bring them in, so that the LORD's community may not be like sheep that have no shepherd." And the LORD answered Moses, "Single out Joshua son of Nun, an inspired man, and lay your hand upon him. Have him stand before Eleazar the priest and before the whole community, and commission him in their sight. Invest him with some of your authority, so that the whole Israelite community may obey. But he shall present himself to Eleazar the priest, who shall on his behalf seek the decision of the Urim before the LORD. By such instruction they shall go out and by such instruction they shall come in, he and all the Israelites, the whole community." Moses did as the LORD commanded him. He took Joshua and had him stand before Eleazar the priest

and before the whole community. He laid his hands upon him and commissioned him—as the LORD had spoken through Moses.[7]

When looking at the verses this way, it is apparent that Moses seeks out the person who will replace him, asking God to make sure the Israelites are not left without a "shepherd." Joshua is ordained in front of the entire community, and he is commissioned by God to replace Moses. The Mosaic dynasty appears to officially end at Numbers 27:12–14, with the commandment for Moses to get ready to die, with God telling him that he will be gathered to his kin:

> The LORD said to Moses, "Ascend these heights of Abarim and view the land that I have given to the Israelite people. When you have seen it, you too shall be gathered to your kin, just as your brother Aaron was. For, in the wilderness of Zin, when the community was contentious, you disobeyed My command to uphold My sanctity in their sight by means of the water." Those are the Waters of Meribath-kadesh, in the wilderness of Zin.[8]

The transition between Numbers 27 and Numbers 28 is awkward at best. From conceivably out of nowhere, the reader sees priestly orders regarding sacrifice, the Sabbath, and the holiday of Shavuot. It can then be inferred that Numbers 28–36 were inserted later to connect in some way to Deuteronomy when it was added later. The redactors needed Moses to still be alive when Numbers ended so that it could connect with Deuteronomy. Biblical aspects of this are important when viewing the Torah as a work of progress, of cutting and pasting, and of redacting as it evolved into the "final" manuscript used today.

It is within this time line of the creation of the Torah that Israelite "myth" evolved into a document of "divine origin" that held historical fact, differentiating itself from the myths and epics of Near Eastern neighbors. The idea that the Torah was divine was actually a late invention and used to provide authority and political gain to those in charge at the time. This was a trend that continued through the Talmudic period, as seen from the verses of Pirkei Avot: "How do we know that Torah is one possession? For it is written, 'The Lord made me as the beginning of His way, the first of His way, the first of His works of old' (Prov 8:22)."[9] Before the Torah became known as divine, the stories existed in the same format as those of the Israelite neighbors in the Near East, oral traditions told around the fire, passed down from generation to generation, as John Van Seters explains:

> Long before nations like Israel and Greece began to write history as a way of explaining the present by references to causes in the past, they had their myths to account for origins. In myth, present reality is based upon what happened to gods and heroes in the primeval time and this establishes an eternal precedent or paradigm. There is an explanation in myth and legend for every custom, institution, and other important aspect of life. . . . They are basically symbolic stories.[10]

It is through this lens that the Torah emerged. This is an important distinction to make when discussing the origin of the Bible, though those who take the now established concept of the Torah's divinity may find it to be impossible to fathom. In response to this, one should remember that unlike in the Hebrew Bible, at least at the end of its canonization process, "divine inspiration" was not even a criterion for canonicity, as it "was developing only during the second century and worked, rather, the other way around. All works of scripture were understood to be divinely inspired, but divine inspiration was never a limiting factor in the establishment of the New Testament."[11]

The "Sister-Wife" Stories in Genesis

There are, truthfully, stories that occur in the Torah (and elsewhere in the Tanakh) that defy logic as to how they ended up in the same volume. The three stories called the "sister-wife" tales within Genesis are a prime example of confusion considering the obvious motif adaption. While these are clear examples of intertextuality—that is, texts "interacting" with one another—for the purposes of our discussion, it is more important to wrestle with the question as to how and why the redactors were unwilling or unable to respond to or redact the presence of all three stories. When viewing them one after another, it becomes intensely difficult to ignore the adaption taking place. We begin with Genesis 12:[12]

There was a famine in the land, and Abram went down to Egypt to sojourn there, for the famine was severe in the land. As he was about to enter Egypt, he said to his wife Sarai, "I know what a beautiful woman you are. If the Egyptians see you, and think, 'She is his wife,' they will kill me and let you live. Please say that you are my sister, that it may go well with me because of you, and that I may remain alive thanks to you." When Abram entered Egypt, the Egyptians saw how very beautiful the woman was. Pharaoh's courtiers saw her and praised her to Pharaoh, and the woman was taken into Pharaoh's palace. And because of her, it went well with Abram; he acquired sheep, oxen, asses, male and female slaves, she-asses, and camels. But Adonai afflicted Pharaoh and his household with mighty plagues on account of Sarai, the wife of Abram. Pharaoh sent for Abram and said, "What is this you have done to me! Why did you not tell me that she was your wife? Why did you say, 'She is my sister,' so that I took her as my wife? Now, here is your wife; take her and be gone!" And Pharaoh put men in charge of him, and they sent him off with his wife and all that he possessed.[13]

The challenge within this story is that of plausibility (i.e., Why is Pharaoh punished when he is innocent? How did he know Abram and Sarai are brother and sister?). It also appears to compromise the character of the matriarch, as the wealth acquired is apparently due to Sarai's beauty and possible sexual favors. These challenges differ from that of the next story, Genesis 20:1–18:

> Abraham journeyed from there to the region of the Negeb and settled between Kadesh and Shur. While he was sojourning in Gerar, Abraham said of Sarah his wife, "She is my sister." So King Abimelech of Gerar had Sarah brought to him. But God came to Abimelech in a dream by night and said to him, "You are to die because of the woman that you have taken, for she is a married woman." Now Abimelech had not approached her. He said, "O Lord, will You slay people even though innocent? He himself said to me, 'She is my sister!' And she also said, 'He is my brother.' When I did this, my heart was blameless and my hands were clean." And God said to him in the dream, "I knew that you did this with a blameless heart, and so I kept you from sinning against Me. That was why I did not let you touch her. Therefore, restore the man's wife—since he is a prophet, he will intercede for you—to save your life. If you fail to restore her, know that you shall die, you and all that are yours." Early next morning, Abimelech called his servants and told them all that had happened; and the men were greatly frightened. Then Abimelech summoned Abraham and said to him, "What have you done to us? What wrong have I done that you should bring so great a guilt upon me and my kingdom? You have done to me things that ought not to be done. What, then," Abimelech demanded of Abraham, "was your purpose in doing this thing?"

"I thought," said Abraham, "surely there is no fear of God in this place, and they will kill me because of my wife. And besides, she is in truth my sister, my father's daughter though not my mother's; and she became my wife. So when God made me wander from my father's house, I said to her, 'Let this be the kindness that you shall do me: whatever place we come to, say there of me: He is my brother.'" Abimelech took sheep and oxen, and male and female slaves, and gave them to Abraham; and he restored his wife Sarah to him. And Abimelech said, "Here, my land is before you; settle wherever you please." And to Sarah he said, "I herewith give your brother a thousand pieces of silver; this will serve you as vindication before all who are with you, and you are cleared before everyone." Abraham then prayed to God, and God healed Abimelech and his wife and his slave girls, so that they bore children; for Adonai had closed fast every womb of the household of Abimelech because of Sarah, the wife of Abraham.[14]

Here we see similar issues, but new questions arise, such as those regarding God's confusion of Abimelech's innocence, as the God in this story does not appear to be omniscient, knowing that Abimelech did not, in fact, sin and yet is punished regardless. Finally, we see the new lead character of Isaac within the same motif in Genesis 26:

There was a famine in the land—aside from the previous famine that had occurred in the days of Abraham—and Isaac went to Abimelech, king of the Philistines, in Gerar. Adonai had appeared to him and said, "Do not go down to Egypt; stay in the land which I point out to you. Reside in this land, and I will be with you and bless you; I will assign all these lands to you and to your heirs, fulfilling the oath that I swore to your father Abraham. I will make your heirs as numerous as the stars of heaven, and assign to your heirs all these lands, so that all the nations of the earth shall bless themselves by your heirs—inasmuch as Abraham obeyed Me and kept My charge: My commandments, My laws, and My teachings." So Isaac stayed in Gerar. When the men of the place asked him about his wife, he said, "She is my sister," for he was afraid to say "my wife," thinking, "The men of the place might kill me on account of Rebekah, for she is beautiful." When some time had passed, Abimelech king of the Philistines, looking out of the window, saw Isaac fondling his wife Rebekah. Abimelech then charged all the people, saying, "Anyone who molests this man or his wife shall be put to death." Abimelech sent for Isaac and said, "So she is your wife! Why then did you say: 'She is my sister?'" Isaac said to him, "Because I thought I might lose my life on account of her." Abimelech said, "What have you done to us! One of the people might have lain with your wife, and you would have brought guilt upon us." Abimelech then charged all the people, saying, "Anyone who molests this man or his wife shall be put to death." Isaac sowed in that land and reaped a hundredfold the same year. Adonai blessed him, and the man grew richer and richer until he was very wealthy: he acquired flocks and herds, and a large household, so that the Philistines envied him. And the Philistines stopped up all the wells which his father's servants had dug in the days of his father Abraham, filling them with earth. And Abimelech said to Isaac, "Go away from us, for you have become far too big for us."

Despite the glaring similarities to the former two stories, this author's goal seems to be to solve some of the issues of the previous narratives, showing his awareness of them. It is also important to note that in this version, God is absent. The three "sister-wife" stories in Genesis 12, 20, and 26 feature a common motif—that is, a pattern or literary structure that can be tracked throughout differing pieces of writing. This particular motif can be summed up as follows:

"A patriarch traveling abroad with his wife attempts to conceal their marital status by claiming that the woman in question is his sister. In each case, the ruse is only partly successful because the wife is coveted by a foreign king, and the resulting complications call into question the moral and ethical character of the ancestors of Israel."[15] Returning to the point of our discussion, how is it possible that when seeing these three stories within the same narrative (Genesis) that one or two were not removed or severely edited to show differences? We are only left with more questions than answers as we dive deeper into the origins and purposes of the stories:

> Succeeding generations of Israelites took care to preserve details about these distinguished families from which they had sprung. But as their descendants continued to retell the tales of the patriarchs far from their time and place of origin, the original significance of wife-sister marriage was forgotten. Because no author of the Torah had access to the social setting of the original story, each one attempted to explain it in a different way. . . . The fact that writers of the Torah preserved traditions they no longer completely understood was a testimony to their trustworthiness and the "general accuracy" of the preserved traditions.[16]

There are, of course, theories as to why situations such as the "sister-wife" tales and others like it (the "rock water" tales within Exod 17:1–7 and Num 20:1–13) coexist in a canonized document. One could make the same argument, perhaps, about why the redactors of the New Testament chose to keep the Synoptic Gospels side by side though their stories differed. In both cases, "canon conscious redactions do not succeed in harmonizing the diverse and even contradictory traditions within the Bible. However, they do enhance the presumption of biblical unity by creating explicit interpretive contexts between books or groups of books."[17]

The Many Manuscripts

In terms of canonization, the most fundamental truth to acknowledge is that the original texts of the Hebrew Bible have never been found. Instead, between the seventh and tenth centuries CE, the Masoretes, a group of scribes, took many manuscripts, including the Ben Asher and the Ben Naphtali scripts, and created an authoritative text. The Ben Asher family of Masoretes, which existed in the Tiberian school, "provided the basis for all printed editions of the Hebrew Bible to this day."[18] The Masoretes were certainly educated and devoted scholars and scribes, but they were also human beings and only could do their best to be consistent with what they knew at the time.

The central manuscript, what we now call the Masoretic Text, or MT, is what is used in Jewish biblical printed texts. But it is important to note that the MT manuscript differs from the texts found at Qumran as part of the Dead Sea Scrolls. It also differs from the manuscript that was used to translate the Bible into Greek, known as the Septuagint. Furthermore, it differs from the Aleppo Codex, the Peshitta, and the Samaritan Pentateuch, and it differs from the manuscript used by the rabbis of the second to fifth century CE in the Mishnah and Talmud. In other words, there has never been a full and consistent biblical text in history. The many differences within the many manuscripts of the Hebrew Bible are best seen in what is known as the *Biblia Hebraica Stuttgartensia*, which allows the reader to see, via codes and notations, the scribal errors, alterations, and distinctions found so far. However, most laypeople do not use this version because it is in Hebrew and because most prefer using one manuscript.

The Greek Septuagint is its own story with regard to the canon. Translated from Hebrew to Greek, the Septuagint's name (Greek for "seventy") comes from a mystical tradition that "seventy-two . . . scholars translated it in Alexandria Egypt" circa third to first century BCE.[19] Two points must be made about this translation: First, the MT was not the manuscript used by the translators of the Septuagint; rather, it appears that those translators used a different manuscript that has now been lost. Second, the Septuagint was used by Christians, specifically Catholics, to create early versions of the Old Testament. Translating directly from the Hebrew text came at a later time.

In any case, the Septuagint was not the only translation used between the second century BCE and fourth century CE. The Hexapla, Aramaic Targumim, Peshitta, and Syriac Christian Old Testament were acknowledged and used throughout that time period, showing once again that the transmission of text was far from linear. However, we do know that the Vulgate, the fourth-century Latin translation of the Bible by Jerome, was created and made official and used by the Catholics as their primary Bible source until the mid-twentieth century.

Today, most English translations of the Bible use the Hebrew text to create versions of the Old Testament—for example, JPS, KJV, ASV, RSV, NRSV, NIV, NAB, and NJB, to name a few. It is important for avid readers of the Bible to see this wide range of translations to see possible nuances in the text.

The Canons

The most common versions of the biblical canon used today are that of the Tanakh, the Roman Catholic and Orthodox Old Testaments, and the Protestant Old Testament. In response to the Roman Catholic Church's Council of Trent in 1546 and its declaration of an official canon, the Protestant churches created their own, with the Presbyterians following "nearly a century later in the Westminster Confession."[20]

A visual representation of these versions of the former is below:[21]

Hebrew Bible	Roman Catholic OT	Protestant OT
Torah	*Pentateuch*	*Pentateuch*
Bereshit	Genesis	Genesis
Sh'mot	Exodus	Exodus
Vayikra	Leviticus	Leviticus
BaMidbar	Numbers	Numbers
D'varim	Deuteronomy	Deuteronomy
Nevi'im	*Historical Books*	*Historical Books*
Joshua	Joshua	Joshua
Judges	Judges	Judges
Samuel 1 and 2	Ruth	Ruth
Kings 1 and 2	Samuel 1 and 2	Samuel 1 and 2
Isaiah	Kings 1 and 2	Kings 1 and 2
Jeremiah	Chronicles 1 and 2	Chronicles 1 and 2
Ezekiel	Ezra[1]	Ezra
The Twelve: Hosea,	Nehemiah	Nehemiah
Joel, Amos, Obadiah,	Tobit	Esther
Jonah, Micah,	Judith	
Nahum, Habakkuk,	Esther[2]	
Zephaniah, Haggai,	1 Maccabees	
Zechariah, Malachi	2 Maccabees[3]	
Ketuvim	*Poetry/Wisdom*	*Poetry/Wisdom*
Psalms	Job	Job
Proverbs	Psalms[4]	Psalms
Job	Proverbs	Proverbs
Song of Songs	Ecclesiastes	Ecclesiastes
Ruth	Song of Solomon	Song of Solomon
Lamentations	Wisdom of Solomon	
Kohelet	Ecclesiasticus (Wisdom of	
(Ecclesiastes)	Sirach)	
Esther		
Daniel		
Ezra-Nehemiah		
Chronicles (1 and 2)		

Hebrew Bible	Roman Catholic OT	Protestant OT
	Prophets	*Prophets*
	Isaiah	Isaiah
	Jeremiah	Jeremiah
	Lamentations	Lamentations
	Baruch[5]	Ezekiel
	Ezekiel	Daniel[7]
	Daniel[6]	The Twelve: Hosea,
	The Twelve: Hosea, Joel,	Joel, Amos, Obadiah,
	Amos, Obadiah, Jonah,	Jonah, Micah, Nahum,
	Micah, Nahum, Habakkuk,	Habakkuk, Zephaniah,
	Zephaniah, Haggai, Zecha-	Haggai, Zechariah,
	riah, Malachi	Malachi
	Apocrypha or Deuterocanon	
	Esdras, Tobit, Judith, addi-	
	tions to Esther, Wisdom	
	of Solomon, Ecclesiastes,	
	Baruch, Letter of Jeremiah,	
	Prayer of Azariah, Susanna,	
	Bel and the Dragon,	
	Prayer of Manasseh, 1 and	
	2 Maccabees	

[1] Greek and Russian Orthodox Bibles also include 1 Esdras, and Russian Orthodox includes 2 Esdras.

[2] With Greek additions.

[3] Greek and Russian Orthodox Bibles include 3 Maccabees.

[4] Greek and Russian Orthodox Bibles include Psalm 151 and the Prayer of
Manasseh.

[5] This includes the Letter of Jeremiah.

[6] With Greek additions.

[7] With Greek additions.

Let us begin this comparison by noting the names of the books and sections in the Hebrew Bible, which are, as to be expected, in Hebrew. As reviewed in the introduction, the Tanakh is a transliterated acronym for Torah (Ta), Nevi'im (na), and Ketuvim (kh), translating to "the Five Books of Moses," "prophets," and "writings," respectively. While all the books of the Hebrew Bible have corresponding Hebrew and English names, I have only selected the Five Books of Moses, as these are the most used and well known. While most of the world is familiar with the Greek or Latin names of the books (Genesis, Exodus, Leviticus, Numbers, and Deuteronomy), you will notice that in the Hebrew Bible, the names of the books are Bereshit, Sh'mot, Vayikra, BaMidbar, and D'varim (transliterated, of course). That is because while the former groupings of names come from translations and reinterpretations of those in the Vulgate, the Hebrew Bible chose to indicate each book the same way it does each *parsha* (section) of the Torah, which is to name that section after its first notable word. For example, the first words of the Hebrew Bible are

בְּרֵאשִׁית בָּרָא אֱלֹהִים

Bereishit bara Elohim (When God began to create)[22]

The word *Bereishit* is the first notable word of that section. We say "notable" word because in the case of Sh'mot, we see the first words of the chapter as

וְאֵלֶּה שְׁמוֹת בְּנֵי יִשְׂרָאֵל

V'ayleh sh'mot b'nai Yisrael (These are the names of the sons of Israel)[23]

As it makes little sense to name a book *V'ayleh* (These are), the name Sh'mot came to be used. The terms *Vayikra*, *BaMidbar*, and *D'varim* are the same format, "He called," "In the Wilderness," and "Words," respectively. As noted above, this is the practice for not just the books of the Torah but also the *parshiot*, the portions selected for each week of reading. The Babylonian practice (now universal) denotes that the Torah is divided into fifty-four sections, which are read every Sabbath (sometimes two at a time, known as "double portions"), allowing the completion of the whole Torah reading in one calendar year. Each *parsha* (section) uses the same system as the chapter names, and each of the fifty-four is named by the first principal word of that section. That being said, with the assimilation of Jews into secular culture, the Greek and Latin names for the Torah books are used quite freely and sometimes more well known.

Another glaring difference seen between Jewish and Christian Bibles is that some of the latter contain books of the Apocrypha in the biblical canon itself. It can also be seen that some of the books within the Catholic Old Testament canons contain "additions" that do not appear in the Hebrew Bible, such as those to Esther and Daniel. These apocryphal books and additions are not included in the Hebrew Bible for various reasons—some theological, some semantic, and some chronological. With these differences now apparent, Christians and Jews alike can recognize that the Hebrew Bible and the Christian Old Testament are not the same.

Key Takeaways from Chapter 4

1. The Hebrew Bible is, assuredly, not the Old Testament (and vice versa). Christian members of the clergy must emphasize

this point over and over to avoid misunderstandings within interfaith communication.

2. The Hebrew Bible was created over centuries (if not longer) with different authors and agendas. The Bible is not a book; it is a library created, in part, through the theological and ideological agenda(s) of the redactors and editors. Parts of the Torah and Tanakh were written at different times and not in the order in which they appear in the final canon. To teach the Hebrew Bible as a chronological history not only is incorrect but leads to a very dangerous path of ignorance and literalism.

3. The Hebrew Bible is organized by Hebrew numbers, chapter names, and *parshiot* (portions). For Christians to learn this would help show more understanding toward the Jewish roots of Christianity.

5

TRANSLATION AND TYPOLOGY

According to *The Guinness Book of World Records*, the Bible, in all its forms, has sold over five billion copies. It is commonly referred to as the best-selling book of all time. The Bible is beloved, cherished, honored, and sometimes even worshipped, what has been defined as "bibliolatry." Bibles can be found in American hotel rooms, pew racks, and store shelves. Copies are carried by missionaries, opened at Bible studies, and quoted on signs carried to sporting events and political rallies. And when these ancient words are read, written, or spoken, it is almost always in that country's vernacular language. The majority of Bibles found in America are in English, just as the majority in Spain are in Spanish. Why? Accessibility to the reader. The drive to learn biblical Hebrew, Greek, and Latin has sadly gone out of style, and most laypersons have not even heard of the influential languages of biblical times, such as Aramaic, Acadian, and Syriac. Translated versions of the Bible have to be printed in the vernacular language of the people, since scholars trained to read the ancient biblical languages are the ones who can actually read the texts. Unfortunately, this means that most Bible readers give little thought to the authenticity of the translation or the translator.

The Trouble with Vowels

It may surprise many readers to discover that biblical Hebrew is a language that was written without vowels, punctuation, accentuation, or any kind of syntax. Rather than noting how a word is to be pronounced or when a sentence is to end, the biblical writers and readers of ancient Hebrew simply knew how or when to do so based on their understanding of the context of the sentence and surrounding words. They also had to rely on those who taught them how to pronounce certain words. This is a practice still used today, for example, in Israeli newspapers written in Modern Hebrew using only the most basic of syntax. Torah scrolls in Jewish synagogues, still handwritten on lamb- or sheepskin, are created without vowels or syntax to present the most authentic-looking Hebrew text when read. It takes a great deal of study and practice to read Hebrew, biblical or otherwise, without the help of vowels to confirm the pronunciation of words. Students learning to read from the Torah often study with what is known as a *tikkun*, a book that features the verses of the Torah on one side as they would appear in the Torah itself (with no vowels or syntax) opposite the verses with vowels and syntax. See figure 1.[1]

On the right side, each word has vowels, known as נִיקוּד (*nikud*), underneath to show its proper pronunciation. Verses are numbered, and there are *trope* marks to show how the Hebrew is to be chanted and where sentences start and stop. On the left is how the Hebrew might appear in the Torah (i.e., no vowels, no verse numbers, no *trope* marks, etc.). The Torah scroll always looks like the Hebrew on the left, and so it was up to a group of scribes (the Masoretes) to create the vowel pointing marks shown on the right. As "universal" as this may appear (because Hebrew words may have similar-looking letter combinations), the addition of vowels to determine which way to

Figure 1

pronounce a word and thus create its meaning was (and still is) a subjective exercise.

In addition to centralizing the text, the Masoretes created manuscripts with vowels and syntax to produce a consistent reading and understanding of the Hebrew. The system of vowels helped promote an easier way of studying and reading both the Torah and the Tanakh. However, the Masoretes encountered words many times in the Torah and Tanakh that looked identical. Without vowels, these words could mean different things if pronounced inconsistently. The Hebrew system of words starts with root letters—usually three letters. Various words are created by adding to the root letters within the same theme. But without the vowels in place, one can only *interpret* the text to mean what they believe it to mean by choosing how to pronounce a word. Let us take some text from the Torah to serve as an example of this problem.

At the end of three verses in the Torah, an identical prohibition appears:[2]

לֹא־תְבַשֵּׁל גְּדִי בַּחֲלֵב אִמּוֹ׃

Lo T'vashayl Ba'chalev Imo

The JPS version translates this sentence as "You shall not boil a kid in its mother's milk." The ESV translates it as "You shall not boil a young goat in its mother's milk." The ASV and KJV, respectively, are relatively close but use Old English: "Thou shalt not boil a kid in its mother's milk; Thou shalt not see a kid in his mother's milk."

I have provided the vowel usage—taken from the *Biblia Hebraica Stuttgartensia*, an edition of the Masoretic Text (MT)—for the word for "milk," here shown as חֲלֵב. The word, according to the MT, is pronounced *cha-layv*. With this vowel usage, the root letters—*chet* (ח), *lamed* (ל), and *vet* (ב)—come together to mean "milk." In the Torah, however, the word would appear simply as חלב, with no vowels to indicate how the word is pronounced. Through research and their own understanding of context, the Masoretes decided that this passage was speaking about milk rather than the other possibilities of these letters in combination—most notably, a word that appears in other verses of the Torah, the Hebrew word for "fat." "Fat" in biblical Hebrew is spelled exactly the same as the word for "milk," only with different vowels. Instead of חֲלֵב (*cha-layv*), with vowels, the word appears as חֵלֶב, pronounced *chay-lev*, as in Exodus 23:18:

לֹא־תִזְבַּח עַל־חָמֵץ דַּם־זִבְחִי וְלֹא־יָלִין חֵלֶב־חַגִּי עַד־בֹּקֶר׃

You shall not offer the blood of My sacrifice with anything leavened; and the **fat** of My festal offering shall not be left lying until morning.[3]

In the Torah, the words for both "milk" and "fat" would appear as חלב, leaving it to the Masoretes to decide exactly in what substance God prohibits a young goat to be boiled. Why is this significant? The former verse became the basis of what is now a universally understood *kashrut* (dietary) law that prohibits the mixing of milk products and meat products in Jewish tradition. The implication of this choice to pronounce the word חלב as *cha-layv* is incredibly vast. One cannot, of course, say that it was the Masoretes who made this choice originally, as this dietary law is discussed far earlier in rabbinic works dating as far back as the second century CE. However, we can, with confidence, state that this was a choice that was made at some point; the Masoretes simply made it official, and it is now commonly interpreted in this way.

This is only one of many examples in biblical Hebrew of words appearing to be identical on the page, so a choice must be made, through context or a certain educational path, to determine how the words are to be pronounced and thus translated. We see from the Masoretes' example that holy text is clearly a product of human choices and interpretations. If the "original" manuscript from which a translation is taken is, in many places, ambiguous, we can see already how the idea of the "perfection" of the Bible begins to slip away.[4]

The Choices by the Translators

Let us discuss for a moment the difficulty of translating words from one language into another. Though not as consistent as our European counterparts, most American middle and high schools require foreign language courses as part of their curricula, offering, at the very least, typically Spanish, German, and French. Other schools, such as the one I attended, offer more, including Latin and Russian. Students are taught how to speak, read, and write in a foreign language, and in the advanced classes, certainly at the university level, they are required to read and translate works of fiction or nonfiction using only their knowledge of the language and perhaps a dictionary as a tool.

I encountered this in French classes at university. When asked to present our work out loud, the professors would always be able to tell who had done their homework, who had attempted to translate that week's assignment, and who had purchased and used an English translation of the French book. How could they tell? Well, for one thing, teachers were most likely familiar with the translation, but more obvious was the fact that French, like any language, is alive and can be translated in many ways. Using the specifically English translation presented only one, though perhaps common, understanding of the French text, while all the other students presented various ways to translate the same sentences. This phenomenon expands far beyond this instance.

How many times have you heard the phrase "There is no English equivalent for this word"? So many words in one language take many words to define, and even when this is done, one can sometimes only produce the gist of the word. For example, the French word *écoeurant* can be explained as "nauseating," but not in the way that would make you physically ill; rather, it refers to a specific type of nausea one only gets when eating foods that are too sweet or rich. There is no one English word equivalent for this type of nausea, and thus it requires an entire sentence just to understand. Another example is the Japanese word *komorebi*, which refers to a particular view of sunlight, specifically when it filters through leaves in a tree. The closest English equivalents might be "sunbeam" or "sun ray," but those do not specifically discuss how the sunlight filters through nature, which is the idea encapsulated in the Japanese word. These instances of complex words and the lack of translatable equivalents occur in biblical Hebrew and in the Bible. Words and phrases in the Hebrew Bible are just as, if not more, difficult to interpret and properly translate into Greek, English, or other vernacular non-Semitic languages.

Most translators are aware of this and are transparent about difficulties they find in the text. However, some problems arise even before the translation occurs. For example, at the bottom of certain pages of the JPS Tanakh, we read the footnote "*meaning of Hebrew uncertain." Similar footnotes are found in various versions of the Bible. This occurs in many forms—sometimes indicating a particular word or set of words is not easy to translate. However, at certain times, this type of footnote occurs in reference to an entire verse. When this happens, the footnote indicates that while the translator can translate each of the words from Hebrew into English, the combination of those words does not seem to make sense in Hebrew, and thus interpretation is necessary. The translator does his or her best to interpret the verse by context or stylistics, but the result is highly subjective. An example is found in Exodus 18:11:

עַתָּה יָדַעְתִּי כִּי־גָדוֹל יְהוָה מִכָּל־הָאֱלֹהִים כִּי בַדָּבָר אֲשֶׁר זָדוּ עֲלֵיהֶם:

The first part of the verse (known as the first stitch) is translatable: "Now I know that the Lord is greater than all gods."[5] However, JPS indicates it is "uncertain" about the second half of the verse (the second stitch). Any biblical Hebrew/English dictionary can help us define all the words in the stitch:

That / because / when (*Ki*)	כִּי
In / at / with word / speech (*Vadavar*)	בַדָּבָר
Which (*Asher*)	אֲשֶׁר
To boil / act presumptuously (*Zadu*)	זָדוּ
Upon / over / above them (*Aleihem*)	עֲלֵיהֶם

With these words, a translator can sense the idea of the stitch but is uncertain as to the proper understanding and meaning of

LET'S TALK

it put together. We can see translators' attempts at this verse and the differing outcomes:

Now I know that the LORD is greater than all gods, yes, by the result of their very schemes against [the people]. (JPS; brackets in the original)

Now I know that Jehovah is greater than all gods; yea, in the thing wherein they dealt proudly against them. (ASV)

Now I know that the LORD is greater than all gods, because in this affair they dealt arrogantly with the people. (ESV)

Now I know that the LORD *is* greater than all gods: for in the thing wherein they dealt proudly *he was* above them. (KJV; my emphasis)

Now I know the LORD is greater than all gods, because he delivered the people from the Egyptians, when they dealt arrogantly with them. (NRSV)[6]

From each translation, a different attempt at this uncertain stitch is born. While the ambiguity of this verse may seem unimportant to some, we should remember the difference between pride (ASV and KJV), arrogance (ESV and NRSV), and schemes (JPS); additionally, it is unclear to whom "them" is referring. JPS and ESV indicate that "them" refers to "people," while KJV and ASV indicate "them" as "gods." NRSV assumes the "them" is the Egyptians. Each choice has strong implications, including determining, perhaps, the personality of God or if there is a divine hierarchy within a group of gods.

This challenge occurs frequently in the Tanakh not only in the form of a sentence or stitch but in the microcosm of words themselves. This literary aspect is known as a hapax legomenon, or "a word or form of which only one instance is recorded in a literature or an author."[7] In reference to the Hebrew Bible, it is also defined more specifically as "any word other than a proper noun which is the only exemplification of its root."[8] As we discussed above in reference to our *cha-layv/chay-lev* argument, Hebrew words contain root letters that shape each various word connected to that root. While a hapax legomenon may share a root with other words in the Bible, its use of vowels, prefixes, and suffixes creates a unique word (i.e., one not used again) in the Hebrew Bible. While the translator can look at other words of the same root to attempt to determine a meaning, some words based on Hebrew root letters have no connection in their meanings. Some instances of a hapax legomenon occur when a word appears only once in the Torah but elsewhere in the Hebrew Bible; however, there are four hundred instances when a word appears only once in the entire canon.

Examples of these *absolute* instances of a hapax legomenon are found in Leviticus, specifically the listing of creatures prohibited by God for the Israelites to eat, Leviticus 11:29–30. In these two verses, four instances of an absolute hapax legomenon appear:

וְזֶה לָכֶם הַטָּמֵא בַּשֶּׁרֶץ הַשֹּׁרֵץ עַל־הָאָרֶץ הַחֹלֶד וְהָעַכְבָּר וְהַצָּב לְמִינֵהוּ׃
וְהָאֲנָקָה וְהַכֹּחַ וְהַלְּטָאָה וְהַחֹמֶט וְהַתִּנְשָׁמֶת׃

These verses list select animals, many of which cannot be determined, as they only appear once in the entire Hebrew Bible. With little to no context, the translators were forced to take literary liberty when attempting to list the animals. We see attempted translations below:[9]

> The following shall be unclean for you from among the things that swarm on the earth: the mole, the mouse, and **great lizards**

of every variety; the **gecko**, the **land crocodile**, the **lizard**, the **sand lizard**, and the chameleon. (JPS)

And these are unclean to you among the swarming things that swarm on the ground: the mole rat, the mouse, the **great lizard** of any kind, the **gecko**, the **monitor lizard**, the **lizard**, the **sand lizard**, and the chameleon. (ESV)

These also *shall be* unclean unto you among the creeping things that creep upon the earth; the weasel, and the mouse, and the **tortoise** after his kind,

And the ferret, and the **chameleon**, and the **lizard**, and the **snail**, and the mole. (KJV)

While KJV seems to have gone in a different direction entirely (including the adding of a species), JPS and ESV do their best to describe kinds of lizards. Interestingly enough, the final word of Leviticus 11:30—וְהַתִּנְשָׁמֶת (*V'hatin'shamet*), translated by JPS and ESV as "chameleon"—is a *dis legomenon* (a word used only twice in the canon), also appearing in Deuteronomy 14:16. This verse appears in another list of prohibited animals for eating, only within the bird variety, and וְהַתִּנְשָׁמֶת is defined in JPS as a completely different species of animal—namely, a white owl: "the little owl, the great owl, and the white owl."[10] Here we can see that within two different chapters and two different contexts, the exact same word, a *dis legomenon*, denotes a completely different meaning in each verse.

In addition to the logistical challenges of translating from Hebrew to the vernacular, there are more intangible tests by the translator of which we should be aware. Translations of the Bible are presented through multiple lenses or levels of free versus literal translation. This happens because Bibles are translated and marketed to specific groups or even age levels. Some translations are intended to be used by academics, and some target lay readers, both Jewish and Christian. Some intentionally choose vocabulary and sentence structures that are at a lower reading level and more suitable for young readers. Each one of these Bible translations carries with it its own theological undertones based on the background of the translators and perhaps to match the intended purpose of and audience for the version. Hebrew Bibles, such as the JPS or ArtScroll versions, are translated by Jewish scholars who have studied the Jewish history of the text.

When we open a translated Bible, we are putting our trust in the translator to provide us with the most authentic understanding of this holy work as seen through their particular theological lenses. David Bellos's book *Is That a Fish in Your Ear? Translation and the Meaning of Everything* provides a list of all that translators do or have the power to do when attempting to translate one text into another. He writes,

> They can replace one word with another of like meaning (synonymy); they can take one part of the expression and replace it with a longer and more elaborate one (expansion); they can take one part of the expression and replace it with a dummy, an abbreviation, a short form, or nothing at all (contraction); they can take one part of the expression and move it to a different position, rearranging the other words in appropriate ways (topic shift); they can use the relevant tool from their language kit to make one part of the expression stand out as more important than others (change of emphasis); they can add expressions that relate to facts of states or opinions implicit in the original in order to clarify what they (or their interlocutor) just said (clarification); but if they try to repeat exactly what has been said with the same tone, pitch, words, forms, and structures,

they do not succeed (unless they are also gifted, sharp-eared, and well-trained impersonators, and probably employed in the music hall).[11]

Translators do the same things when they approach biblical texts. For example, take the issue of the subconscious (or conscious) inserting of one's culture into his or her translation work. A Jewish author, translator, or redactor may look at the text and, through the lens of his or her theology, interpret it one way. A Christian author may do the same, interpreting it more in line with his or her belief system. This, as Michel Foucault explains, is unavoidable, as he writes, "One is admitting that there must be a level (as deep as it is necessary to imagine it) at which the *oeuvre* emerges, in all its fragments, even the smallest, most inessential ones, as the expression of the thought, the experience, the imagination, or the unconscious of the author, or, indeed, of the historical determinations that operated upon him."[12] In other words, when we read a translation, we are also reading that translator's interpretation of the Bible, which is based on their experience, culture, language, and thought process. While certain passages in both Testaments can be universally agreed upon to mean the same thing, some instances of ambiguity can have drastic consequences.

Take, for instance, the famous verse of Isaiah 7:14, which has traditionally been understood by many Christians to predict the coming of their Christ:

לָכֵן יִתֵּן אֲדֹנָי הוּא לָכֶם אוֹת הִנֵּה הָעַלְמָה הָרָה וְיֹלֶדֶת בֵּן וְקָרֵאת שְׁמוֹ
עִמָּנוּ אֵל:

Let us begin by juxtaposing two common translations, one Jewish and one Christian:

Assuredly, my Lord will give you a sign of His own accord!
Look, the *young woman* is with child and about to give birth to
a son. Let her name him Immanuel. (JPS)[13]

Therefore the Lord himself shall give you a sign; Behold, a
virgin shall conceive, and bear a son, and shall call his name
Immanuel. (KJV)[14]

The question here is how to properly translate the Hebrew
word הָעַלְמָה, pronounced *HaAlmah*. The Hebrew meaning of
this word is commonly understood by Jewish scholars as "young
woman" or "maiden." This can be determined by the use of
the word in other contexts, such as Genesis 24:43 and Exodus 2:8,
which both, by context, seem to indicate a girl or a young woman:

הִנֵּה אָנֹכִי נִצָּב עַל־עֵין הַמָּיִם וְהָיָה **הָעַלְמָה** הַיֹּצֵאת לִשְׁאֹב וְאָמַרְתִּי
אֵלֶיהָ

הַשְׁקִינִי־נָא מְעַט־מַיִם מִכַּדֵּךְ:

As I stand by the spring of water, let the *young woman* who
comes out to draw and to whom I say, "Please, let me drink a
little water from your jar."[15]

וַתֹּאמֶר־לָהּ בַּת־פַּרְעֹה לֵכִי וַתֵּלֶךְ **הָעַלְמָה** וַתִּקְרָא אֶת־אֵם הַיָּלֶד:

And Pharaoh's daughter answered, "Yes." So the *girl* went and
called the child's mother.[16]

Further, Jewish scholars (and lay Jews) understand Isaiah
7:14 to be a metaphor for circumstances during Isaiah's time;

in Jewish tradition, it is not perceived as a premonition. One of the most famous and trusted Jewish commentators, Shlomo Yitzchaki, the twelfth-century French Jewish sage known as Rashi, explains the verse this way:

> **Immanuel** [lit. "God is with us." That is] to say that our Rock shall be with us, and this is the sign, for she is a young girl, and she never prophesied, yet in this instance, Divine inspiration shall rest upon her. This is what is stated below (8:3): "And I was intimate with the prophetess, etc.," and we do not find a prophet's wife called a prophetess unless she prophesied. Some interpret this as being said about Hezekiah, but it is impossible, because, when you count his years, you find that Hezekiah was born nine years before his father's reign. And some interpret that this is the sign, that she was a young girl and incapable of giving birth.[17]

When the Tanakh was translated from a Hebrew manuscript into Greek (the Septuagint) between the third and first centuries BCE, the translators had to do the difficult task of taking the fluid language (as described above) of Hebrew and translating it into Greek. As stated previously, there are many difficulties in translating from one language to another, the least of which is the challenge of finding new equivalent words to capture the meaning of the word to be translated. The translators of the Septuagint attempted to find a word in Greek to fit the Hebrew word of *almah*. The choice the translators made was the Greek word παρθένος, pronounced *parthenos*. *Parthenos* is not as ambiguous a word for maiden as *almah*, and in Greek, the word literally carries the meaning of a woman who has not had sexual intercourse—that is, a virgin.

One cannot fault the translators of the Septuagint for theological bias, since Christianity did not exist between the third and first centuries BCE, when the translation was done; in fact, Jesus is said to have been born in the first century CE, hundreds of years later. However, the implications of this interpretation, changing "maiden" to "virgin," quickly came to be extremely significant when the Gospels were written, and heavy work of typology (which we will discuss further) was done to create the impression that prophecies from the Old Testament pointed forward to the New Testament.

Many Christian Bible versions—such as the KJV, ASV, and ESV, though translated directly from the Hebrew MT—all feature the choice of "virgin" over "maiden" or "young girl," while others, such as the NRSV, CEB, and Good News (TEV), use "young woman." Early on, the Septuagint became widely accepted in Christian circles, and translators could not shake its influence. Some Christian translations have retained "virgin" in the text because this was the centuries-old tradition. Some fear that losing the specific term dilutes the Christian understanding of Jesus's mother, Mary, being a virgin who conceived by the power of the Holy Spirit. Could it be argued that the instances of "young girl" in both the Isaiah verse and the Genesis and Exodus verses should carry the assumption that the young girl is a virgin? Perhaps. But the Greek *parthenos* emphasizes what is an unimportant aspect of the word, causing a massive reinterpretation of the text that is part of the core theology of Christianity, now over one billion strong.

Another example with far worse implications and consequences from differing translations comes from the verses of Exodus 34:34–35:

Whenever Moses went in before the LORD to speak with Him, he would leave the veil off until he came out; and when he came out and told the Israelites what he had been commanded, the Israelites would see how radiant the skin of Moses' face was.

Moses would then put the veil back over his face until he went in to speak with Him.

The word in question is the Hebrew term for "radiant" or "shining" referring to the skin of Moses's face. The word in Hebrew in this case is קָרַן (*karan*). While this might seem like an arbitrary verse and word, a fourth-century Christian translator, Eusebius Sophronius Hieronymus, also known as Saint Jerome, brought much controversy to the subject. In translating the Hebrew text to Latin in the Vulgate, he mistranslated the Hebrew word *karan* (radiance) for קֶרֶן, pronounced *keren* and meaning "horn." This mistaken translation from a misreading of the Hebrew vowels led to the view that Moses was "horned," which sadly inspired Christian artists such as Michelangelo and Donatello to portray Moses as having horns in their art. The ramifications of this led to a faulty interpretation by some Christians that Jews, like "devils" or "demons," had horns and thus were the embodiment of the Gospel of John's description of Jews being the offspring of the "father of lies."[18] As one can imagine, the anti-Semitic prejudice, discrimination, torture, and murder in response to this Christian understanding are incalculable. It is examples like this that demonstrate the heavy weight of translations and their ramifications.

So we can track the translations of words in a Hebrew manuscript to another language and note that they can differ. We can also engage in an exercise that does the reverse; by looking at how a translation came to be, we can see why a particular word or passage was translated as such and how it may differ from the more common manuscript source. A notable example is Deuteronomy 32:6–9. The context of the passage is Moses's last speeches to the Israelites before his death. Moses speaks to the crowd in front of him, telling them to remember the days of the ancestors, when God divided up the peoples and fixed the boundaries of peoples. The JPS translation, starting from Deuteronomy 32:6, provides the following:

> *Do you thus requite the LORD [Yahweh], O dull and witless*
> *people? Is not He the Father who created you—*
> *Fashioned you and made you endure!*
> *Remember the days of old, Consider the years of ages past; Ask*
> *your father, he will inform you, Your elders, they will tell*
> *you: When the Most High [Elyon] gave nations their homes*
> *And set the divisions of man, He fixed the boundaries of*
> *peoples In relation to Israel's numbers. For the LORD's*
> *[Yahweh's] portion is His people, Jacob His own allotment.*[19]

It is important to note that God is referred to in two different ways in the two verses of Deuteronomy 32:8–9. God is called Elyon, which JPS translates as "the Most High," and the Tetragrammaton, the unpronounceable name of God, spelled *yud*, *hay*, *vav*, *hay* (יהוה), which for our purposes, we will pronounce as "Yahweh" in order to remove any theological aspects of the textual analysis. While some in religious settings might refer to the Tetragrammaton as "Adonai," "God," or "Hashem," by using "Yahweh," we leave it open to interpretation.

The discrepancy that arises when analyzing this passage occurs in the last words of Deuteronomy 32:8. The MT states the following:

בְּהַנְחֵל עֶלְיוֹן גּוֹיִם בְּהַפְרִידוֹ בְּנֵי אָדָם יַצֵּב גְּבֻלֹת עַמִּים לְמִסְפַּר **בְּנֵי יִשְׂרָאֵל**

According to the MT, Deuteronomy 32:8 provides the ending of that sentence as בְּנֵי יִשְׂרָאֵל, pronounced *b'nai Yisrael*. A common translation might be "the children of Israel" or simply

"Israelites," as the "*b'nai*" is understood to stand in for "the people of," such as in Genesis 36:31:

וְאֵ֣לֶּה הַמְּלָכִ֗ים אֲשֶׁ֤ר מָלְכוּ֙ בְּאֶ֣רֶץ אֱד֔וֹם לִפְנֵ֥י מְלָךְ־מֶ֖לֶךְ לִ**בְנֵ֥י יִשְׂרָאֵֽל**

These are the kings who reigned in the land of Edom before any king reigned over the Israelites.[20]

With this in mind, we can now refer back to Deuteronomy 32:8–9 and the discrepancy at hand. When we read the verses in Hebrew or the English translation, the concepts are difficult to understand. Let us first analyze it in translation:

When Elyon gave nations as an inheritance, and when he separated the sons of man, he set the boundaries of the peoples according to the number of the sons of Israel.[21]

This passage is discussing the separation of humans into tribes, each one receiving an inherited set of lands. However, the ending makes little sense. How could God set the boundaries of peoples according to the sons of Israel? The verse uses the term גּוֹיִ֑ם (pronounced *goyim*), meaning "nations," and refers to a group of people other than the Israelites. These tribes, or peoples, such as Canaanites, Amorites, and Hittites, would not be divided according to the number of Israelites.

However, we discover some clarity for this confusing verse when we read the translation of Deuteronomy 32:8–9 in the Septuagint and the same verse taken from the recovered book of Deuteronomy found in the Qumran Dead Sea Scrolls (4QDeut). The Septuagint translation reads as follows:

When the Most High divided the nations, when he separated the sons of Adam, he set the boundaries of the nations, according to the number of the angels of God (*aggelón theou*). And his people Jacob became the portion of the Lord, Israel was the line of his inheritance.

Here the *b'nai Yisrael*, "the children of Israel" in the MT, appears as *aggelón theou*, or "angels of God." That is quite a leap—to go from the discussion of a people, here the Israelite tribes, to the angels of God. Because this translation is too far of a leap to be a mistake, scholars dug deeper to find out what truly was happening here. When we look at the verses as found in the Dead Sea Scrolls, shown below in the translation, we find that the Hebrew in that manuscript corresponds to the translation found within the Septuagint:

When Elyon gave the nations as an inheritance, when he separated the sons of man, he set the boundaries of the peoples according to the number of gods. (4QDeut)

In the Dead Sea Scrolls' manuscript, *b'nai Yisrael* appears as *b'nai elohim*. The 4QDeut manuscript predates the MT and the Septuagint, making it the oldest of the three, and it contains something entirely different theologically. *B'nai elohim*, which can be translated as "children of gods" or "people of gods," is better translated simply as "gods," just as we saw above that *b'nai Yisrael* was not "the children of Israel" but simply "Israel." According to this older translation, the verse begins to take shape through the lens of monolatry, the "belief in the existence of many gods but with the consistent worship of only one deity."[22] This belief, which differs from monotheism, is the acceptance that all peoples have their own gods and the understanding that the god one tribe worships may be believed to be more powerful than another. Two of the most prominent examples of monolatry in the Tanakh are Exodus 15:11 (the Song of the Sea) and Micah 4:5:

מִי־כָמֹכָה בָּאֵלִם יְהֹוָה מִי כָּמֹכָה נֶאְדָּר בַּקֹּדֶשׁ נוֹרָא תְהִלֹּת עֹשֵׂה פֶלֶא

Who is like You among the gods, Yahweh? Who is like You,
majestic in holiness, awesome in splendor, working wonders![23]

כִּי כָּל־הָעַמִּים יֵלְכוּ אִישׁ בְּשֵׁם אֱלֹהָיו וַאֲנַחְנוּ נֵלֵךְ בְּשֵׁם־יְהֹוָה אֱלֹהֵינוּ
לְעוֹלָם וָעֶד:

Though all the peoples walk each in the names of its gods, We
will walk in the name of Yahweh, our God Forever and ever.[24]

With this basic understanding of monolatry, we can now see
that Deuteronomy 32:8–9 is explaining that Elyon divided up all
of the peoples on earth and provided gods for each of the groups
created; the following verse (v. 10) tells us that Yahweh received His
portion, which was His people, the followers of Jacob (Israelites).

Cultural Repertoire

We talked earlier about the belief held by some that the words
of the Torah and the Bible are perfect and "eternal," meaning
that the words and lessons found within transcend time and
societal limits. But a look at the history of biblical interpretation
reveals just how rigid some views of the meanings of Scriptures
can be. This may pertain to the laws in the Torah or the teachings of the Gospels. A literalist belief system maintains that the
moral understandings within the Bible are constant and do not
reflect the evolution of humanity. Proponents of this belief system have used biblical texts that appear to support slavery, the
submissive role of women, and the prohibition of homosexuality
to apply those matters to the present day as strongly as they were
at the time the texts were created. Such a belief system can provide problems and inconsistencies when used to enforce biblical

laws or turn them into modern ones. Take, for instance, the laws of Deuteronomy 22:23–26:

> In the case of a virgin who is engaged to a man—if a man comes upon her in town and lies with her, you shall take the two of them out to the gate of that town and stone them to death: the girl because she did not cry for help in the town, and the man because he violated another man's wife. Thus you will sweep away evil from your midst. But if the man comes upon the engaged girl in the open country, and the man lies with her by force, only the man who lay with her shall die, but you shall do nothing to the girl. The girl did not incur the death penalty, for this case is like that of a man attacking another and murdering him.

While certain members of cultures, even in the twenty-first century, may believe that a woman is at fault when she is raped, it can be safely stated that society as a whole has moved away from the belief thanks to the education about rape culture, and laws that have been enacted in most countries reflect this change. I have yet to hear a strong argument that these laws from Deuteronomy should be eternal laws meant to fit in any period or any society.

This example stands with many others in both the Hebrew Bible and the New Testament. We also recognize the problematic laws regarding the ownership of another human being as property as well as the understanding of women as the property of their fathers until they are married, when they then become the property of their husbands. Other passages in the Tanakh are equally disturbing. Joshua's attack on Jericho ends with the extermination of everything in the city, men and women, young and old, ox and sheep and ass. Jewish prophets have some problematic speeches, including Joel's reversal of the common vision of peace, stating, "Beat your plowshares into swords, and your pruning hooks into spears."[25] Slavery, patriarchal favoritism, sanctioned murder, rape, thievery, and genocide all stand prominently on the pages of our Scriptures.

Those in pastoral and priestly roles can choose to ignore these problematic texts, perhaps by refusing to speak about them when they appear in the biblical reading cycle, but this reflects a "bury your head in the sand" approach. We cannot change the canon, much as many would like to, so instead, we must analyze the presence of these problematic and morally challenging rules and regulations of biblical life.

A term that I believe we must familiarize ourselves with when reading the Bible or any work written at a different time than our own is *cultural repertoire*. This perspective, discussed by multiple scholars in various fields, is described by Karri Holley as follows:

> Culture consists of a repertoire of behaviors that includes symbols of meaning and practices selectively used by group members to construct "strategies of action." From this definition, culture can be seen in a causal role; that is, the strategies of action pursued by group members are cultural products. Individuals pursue such strategies within unique social contexts, which influence decision making and behavior. The ritualistic practices and symbolic meanings held by a group provide individuals a means to organize reality.[26]

Holley also does a commendable job in defining for us the components of cultural repertoire, which are semiotic codes, collective schemas, hierarchy of practices, and communities. Semiotic codes can be defined as "relationships of meaning that are associated with institutional arrangements"; collective schemas as "widely understood and shared templates that provide guidelines for behavior; enacted through public rituals and transmitted"; hierarchy of practices as "relationships between various practices; some cultural practices organize, define, or constrain others"; and communities as "utilization of cultural repertoire develops identity, which is reinforced by participation in community of practice."[27]

In other words, whenever we read a piece of writing from a certain culture other than our own, we should be aware of the heavy amounts of influence, listed above, that affect the author's work (though perhaps we should do this for writing from our own culture as well). We should also be aware that our own cultural influences provide lenses for reading the works of other cultures. These lenses contain our own subconscious biases, our thoughts created by experiences, and our understandings based on the influences we have received from our family, friends, school, location, time period, and most importantly for our current discussion, religion.

Therefore, when we analyze a writing by an author from another time period and another culture, we must do our best to remove these lenses in order to step into the shoes of the writer. It is imperative that we understand the author's cultural repertoire before we can even begin to interpret his or her work. For fear that we will make wildly inaccurate observations, we cannot read Shakespeare, for example, and understand the humor, idioms, or concerns of the characters unless we study the period and culture in which Shakespeare is said to have lived. While we may not be aware, we are currently shaping our own cultural repertoire. Indeed, this book you are reading is fraught with twenty-first-century Jewish semiotic codes and collective schemas. Michel Foucault describes this phenomenon this way: "We are not even sure of ourselves when we use these distinctions in our own world of discourse, let alone when we are analyzing groups of statements which, when first formulated, were distributed, divided, and characterized in a quite different way."[28]

Each choice of word or phrasing an author makes comes from a source within that has shaped their analyses of situations and their recording of historical events. Just as we are susceptible to the influence of cultural repertoire, we must realize that so too were the authors of the Torah, the Hebrew Bible, and the New Testament.

Typology

During my days in seminary, I would travel to small counties in Ohio to do presentations on Judaism for churches and Christian communities. Often the groups were extremely gracious and only accidentally insulting, such as when one of the participants at one gathering said to me, "When the Jews are worried about the economy, I know to be worried." I spent the majority of the sessions detailing the basics of the Torah, the Tanakh, and Jewish theology and philosophy and perhaps discussing the politics of the State of Israel. However, the most common question I received, in some form or another, basically was, "How can you ignore all the signs in the Old Testament that predict Jesus?" At the time, I knew the basics about the topic, but I never had a satisfying answer, though I probably wouldn't have no matter what. But having now studied in detail both the Hebrew Bible and the New Testament as well as biblical criticism and the like, I am more than prepared to answer the question, which is one that many lay Christians may be too hesitant to ask of Jews.

I think it best to begin with the suggestion that if you are to ask this question of Jews, the phrasing is important. Obviously, the gentleman who asked me "How can you ignore all the signs in the Old Testament that predict Jesus?" was asking in an accusatory and somewhat condescending way. A better way to ask would be, "We Christians see predictions of Jesus in the Hebrew Bible; what are your thoughts on that topic?" That kind of question acknowledges that we may (and do) share different understandings and wish no disrespect to one another. Of course, you may receive different kinds (and lengths) of answers when asking this question of Jews, even respectfully. I suggest asking a rabbi or biblical scholar rather than a Jewish layperson, as the correctness of the answer is as important as the question. One simple, short answer to the question—"Is not Jesus predicted in your (Jewish) Bible?"[29]—comes (with my thanks) from a teacher of mine:

> No. We would need to see his name. As for motifs that you may claim point to Jesus, Gospel writers likely conformed Jesus' image expressly to match these motifs, so your citing them would be circular reasoning. Moreover, we are not dependent solely on ancient texts but also on later revised interpretations and understandings that constantly renew our religion and keep it up to date.[30]

This answer provides solutions to several issues. It brings about the very important point that biblical authors were not parsimonious about using names in the Hebrew Bible—that is, male names, at least. A quick review of any section of the Hebrew Bible shows an abundance (if not overabundance) of the names of people and places. Even in the so-called Christian predictive texts, the names never lead to Jesus, such as in Isaiah 7:14: "Look, the young woman is with child and about to give birth to a son. Let her name him Immanuel."[31] "Immanuel" is not the name "Jesus," nor is there any other example of a name meaning another name in all of Hebrew Scripture. This, of course, is a simplistic view of a highly developed and institutionalized theological understanding by Christians called biblical typology:

> Typology is a method of biblical interpretation whereby an element found in the Old Testament is seen to prefigure one found in the New Testament. The initial one is called the

type and the fulfillment is designated the *antitype*. Either type or antitype may be a person, thing, or event, but often the type is messianic and frequently related to the idea of salvation.[32]

In other words, *typology* is the act of looking back at the Hebrew Bible and finding parallels or "predictors" in the New Testament. Let me explain why such biblical typology is problematic for Jews. There are examples in the Gospels and New Testament that parallel genres and verses from the Hebrew Bible. These "parallels" are based on New Testament authors making strategic decisions to connect the writings of the Hebrew Bible to what would be the "new" stories. As we spoke about in chapter 1, because the Gospels were written at least forty years after the historic accounts of the life of Jesus, the Gospel writers were writing stories that were two generations old. Without a full chronology of Jesus's life or witnesses present at the events or records of dialogues and sermons, they filled those chronological holes with what they knew (the stories of the Hebrew Bible) in ways that supported their stories, creating meaning for the followers. They knew the Hebrew Bible in full, canonized in the first century BCE, which means that any Hebrew Scripture "parallels" seen in the New Testament are there by design. Gospel writers, for example, intentionally used the verses and themes of the Hebrew Bible to shape the New Testament. For example, note Zechariah 9:9 in the Hebrew Bible:

> Rejoice greatly, Fair Zion; Raise a shout, Fair Jerusalem! Lo, your king is coming to you. He is victorious, triumphant, yet humble, riding on an ass, on a donkey foaled by a she-ass.

Within both Judaism and Christianity, this verse is perceived to be a premonition of the coming of a messianic figure. Rashi, our twelfth-century French Jewish teacher, comments on the verse:

Behold! Your king shall come to you—It is impossible to interpret this except as referring to the King Messiah, as it is stated: "and his rule shall be from sea to sea." We do not find that Israel had such a ruler during the days of the Second Temple.[33]

The rabbis of the Talmud also agreed that this verse was important in regard to the coming of the Messiah:

Rabbi Alexandri says: Rabbi Yehoshua ben Levi raises a contradiction between two depictions of the coming of the Messiah. It is written: "There came with the clouds of heaven, one like unto a son of man . . . and there was given him dominion and glory and a kingdom . . . his dominion is an everlasting dominion" (Daniel 7:13–14). And it is written: "Behold, your king will come to you; he is just and victorious; lowly and riding upon a donkey and upon a colt, the foal of a donkey" (Zechariah 9:9). Rabbi Alexandri explains: If the Jewish people merit redemption, the Messiah will come in a miraculous manner with the clouds of heaven. If they do not merit redemption, the Messiah will come lowly and riding upon a donkey.[34]

It was verses like this that were used to build the archetype of the Messiah image that the New Testament writers created for Jesus. Specifically, we see Jesus as that messianic figure in the Gospel of John:

The next day the great crowd that had come for the festival heard that Jesus was on his way to Jerusalem. They took palm branches and went out to meet him, shouting, "Hosanna!" "Blessed is he who comes in the name of the Lord!" "Blessed is the king of Israel!" Jesus found a young donkey and sat on it, as it is written: "Do not be afraid, Daughter Zion; see, your king is coming, seated on a donkey's colt."[35]

The author of the Gospel of John is fully aware of the imagery in Zechariah and projects it onto Jesus. We see the same practice used in Zechariah 13:

> O sword! Rouse yourself against My shepherd, The man in charge of My flock—says the LORD of Hosts. Strike down the shepherd And let the flock scatter; And I will also turn My hand Against all the shepherd boys.[36]

This passage has a parallel biblical typology in the Gospel of Mark:

> "You will all fall away," Jesus told them, "for it is written: 'I will strike the shepherd, and the sheep will be scattered.'"[37]

Jesus here is quoting Zechariah 13:7 as part of his prediction of Peter's denial:

> "But after I have risen, I will go ahead of you into Galilee." Peter declared, "Even if all fall away, I will not." "Truly I tell you," Jesus answered, "today—yes, tonight—before the rooster crows twice you yourself will disown me three times." But Peter insisted emphatically, "Even if I have to die with you, I will never disown you." And all the others said the same.[38]

The author of Mark uses this verse from the prophet to project Jesus as a messianic figure. We see the same process occurring in Zechariah 11:

> Then I said to them, "If you are satisfied, pay me my wages; if not, don't." So they weighed out my wages, thirty shekels of

silver—the noble sum that I was worth in their estimation. The LORD said to me, "Deposit it in the treasury." And I took the thirty shekels and deposited it in the treasury in the House of the LORD.[39]

The Gospel of Matthew quotes Zechariah at this point, using these images to describe the betrayal of Judas:

The chief priests picked up the coins and said, "It is against the law to put this into the treasury, since it is blood money." So they decided to use the money to buy the potter's field as a burial place for foreigners. That is why it has been called the Field of Blood to this day. Then what was spoken by Jeremiah the prophet was fulfilled: "They took the thirty pieces of silver, the price set on him by the people of Israel, and they used them to buy the potter's field, as the Lord commanded me."[40]

First, it is important to note that the author of Matthew makes a mistake here, as it is not Jeremiah who states these words but Zechariah. This should be troubling enough, but again, the strategy is intended to signal to the reader of the Gospel that something is happening here that echoes the prophetic works of the Hebrew Bible.

When serving as a hospital chaplain, I received a Christian pocket collection of liturgy, including the Psalms. When I came to Psalm 22, the book labeled it as "Jesus' prayer on the cross." I found myself vexed, since I knew Psalm 22 to have been written long before the writer of Mark used the words to parallel the psalm. Verses 1, 6, 16, and 18 in Psalm 22 match up almost exactly to verses 34, 29, and 24 of Mark 15, as seen in the following table:[41]

Psalm 22 (BCE)	Mark 15 (ca. 72 CE)
1. My God, my God why hast thou forsaken me? . . .	34. Jesus cried . . . , "My God, my God, why hast thou forsaken me?"
6. Scorned by men, . . . despised by the people. All . . . mock at me . . . wag their heads . . .	29. . . . those who passed by derided him, wagging their heads . . .
16. . . . evildoers encircle me; they have pierced my hands and feet . . .	24. And they crucified him,
18. They divide my garments among them, . . . for my raiment they cast lots . . .	And divided his garments among them, casting lots for them . . .

The author of Mark's Gospel clearly uses Psalm 22 as a lens to interpret the death of Jesus, including having him say words from the psalm on the cross. This typology and parallelism are reminiscent of a modern-day remix in which a musical artist takes the "hook" or baseline or musical score from one song and uses it as the basis of their own musical creation, thus creating new music inspired by the old. For Jews, this type of remixing signals a kind of "ownership" of the original (Hebrew) text. The new recording is not the old, but by shaping it in a new way, it can seem as if the original is being co-opted for a purpose that was not originally intended. And when the remix claims to "replace" the original, it feels as if the original is devalued.

A pattern of paralleling Jesus as an archetype of Moses can be found throughout the Gospel of Matthew. These parallels include an infancy narrative, a temptation in the wilderness, the giving of the law, and a transfiguration on a mountain.[42] While some readers may pick up on this literary motif adaption immediately and some may not notice until it is pointed out, most important for our discussion is the fact that this is a literary device used to show Jesus as conforming to Moses. Again, because the books of the Torah (and Joshua) were well known and available to the Gospel writers, it is not surprising that such comparisons would be made, especially if the primary audience for Matthew's Gospel were Jews who had questions about who Jesus was.

And what of the "suffering servant" from Isaiah 53, which has attracted incredible attention from Jewish and Christian scholars alike?

> Who can believe what we have heard? Upon whom has the arm of the LORD been revealed? For he has grown, by His favor, like a tree crown, Like a tree trunk out of arid ground. He had no form or beauty, that we should look at him: No charm, that we should find him pleasing. He was despised, shunned by men, A man of suffering, familiar with disease. As one who hid his face from us, He was despised, we held him of no account. Yet it was our sickness that he was bearing, Our suffering that he endured. We accounted him plagued, Smitten and afflicted by God; But he was wounded because of our sins, Crushed because of our iniquities.[43]

The key question about this text is, Who is the servant? This passage—which is known to come from Deutero-Isaiah, meaning from the second author of the book of Isaiah, a work written later than the first chapters—"generally refers to the nation as a whole or an idealized representation of the nation."[44] In other words, the "suffering servant" is most likely the nation of Israel, not a specific person. Some rabbinic texts do suggest the servant is a messianic figure, but most scholars believe this to be unlikely, as "nowhere else does Deutero-Isaiah refer to the Messiah, and the absence of a belief in an individual Messiah is one of the hallmarks of Deutero-Isaiah's outlook (in contrast to that of First Isaiah)."[45]

Some commentators believe the character refers to later prophets such as Jeremiah,[46] but the rabbis of the Talmud identified the suffering servant as Moses:

> The Holy One, Blessed be He, said to him: Do you seek to enter the land to perform these mitzvot for any reason other than to receive a reward? I will ascribe you credit as if you had performed them and you will receive your reward, as it is stated: "Therefore will I divide him a portion among the great, and he shall divide the spoil with the mighty; because he bared his soul unto death, and was numbered with the transgressors; yet he bore the sin of many, and made intercession for the transgressors" (Isaiah 53:12).[47]

A great deal of work has been done by rabbis and Jewish biblical scholars to refute the idea that the "suffering servant" refers to Jesus. Christians have often interpreted the suffering servant as an archetype that points to Jesus. An example of an article that simply goes too far, in my opinion, is written by Hope Bolinger for Christianity.com:

> Could it Be Someone Else? Not likely. Many Jewish scholars struggle with this passage because it clearly points to Jesus. Although they've offered other contenders such as Isaiah, Jeremiah, or even the Jewish people. After all, throughout their history, Jews have been despised and rejected. However, none of the contenders appear to fit the substitutionary roles the suffering servant plays. None of those contenders can heal us by their wounds and restore us to God.[48]

It is interpretations like this that lead Jews to be frustrated by the exercise of "prophetic" biblical typologies. While viewing synagogues in South Carolina as part of a trip on the origins of southern Jewry, I engaged in a conversation with a Christian about the problematic aspects of typology. It was difficult for him to understand why it was bothersome to Jews, and so I was able to work my way through a metaphor. I asked him if he had ever heard the song "Smooth Criminal." He said he had, and I asked if he knew who performed it. "Easy," he said, "Michael Jackson." I said, "Right, but do you also remember the cover version that hit the radio waves in 2001 by a band called Alien Ant Farm?" He said he remembered, to which I explained the metaphor: "Smooth Criminal" was written by Michael Jackson and produced by Quincy Jones in 1987.[49] Alien Ant Farm's version came out in 2001, fourteen years later. When Alien Ant Farm's version hit the radio waves, there were children around the world who had never heard Michael Jackson's version. When asked who wrote the song, they would reply, "Alien Ant Farm," having no idea it was a cover. I told the Christian man, "Now imagine that those children told you that the Alien Ant Farm version of 'Smooth Criminal' was the 'true' version, that Michael Jackson wrote the song *as a prophecy for* Alien Ant Farm so they could top the charts, and that Alien Ant Farm miraculously composed the same song—with a few differences."[50] The Christian man was astounded. He said he'd never accept that and that someone would need to just tell those kids who wrote the original song and what Michael Jackson's original inspiration was.

Therein lies the issue Jews take with typology. When there is a "remix" or "cover" of Hebrew Bible texts, it is done intentionally for a different agenda. To say that those older texts in the Hebrew Bible *predicted* or were written *for* the events in the New Testament removes the original contexts and meanings behind them. This practice can feed the anti-Jewish trope that Christians know and understand Jewish texts better than Jews

themselves do. It serves Christians well to be aware of the problematic aspects of typology and how this can lead to supersessionism rather than a respect for Jewish biblical interpretation.

Key Takeaways from Chapter 5

1. The Bible, both the Hebrew Scriptures and the Christian
   Bible, is the product of human redactors and translators.
   We have shown how the translation of ancient texts into
   English or other modern languages is not a simple one-step
   process. Translators are removed from the texts' original
   contexts, and they have their own agendas and theological
   biases. This should make us both humble and a bit wary as
   we read any translation.

2. Those who interpret the words of the Bible in a way that
   is "timeless" forget that they are only interpreting the
   meanings behind the words by retrospective translation.
   We cannot possibly understand fully the culture in which
   these documents were written, despite our ability to study it
   extensively.

3. From the modern Jewish perspective, considering that the
   Gospel writers had no way of knowing the birth or life story
   of Jesus in full, the followers of Jesus used a motif, the outline of the hero of the Hebrew Bible (Moses), and put it
   into place for their own hero, Jesus; in addition, the Gospel
   writers used common and understood literary tropes from
   the Hebrew Bible in order to make the Jesus narrative more
   authentic in its "premonition" of things to come. Modern
   Jews recognize this and thus disagree with the usage of
   Hebrew Bible texts in this way.

4. Certainly, we understand that writers have intents,
   motives, and messages to get through and that they can

use poetic license to change a few details or hyperbolize others. The questions to ask a congregation are, What do we as modern Christians do with this information or with more information like it? How would it affect our view of the Gospels?

6

EASY ANSWERS TO
EIGHTEEN BIG QUESTIONS

Most questions about religion are not easily answered by brief answers, but simple responses to big questions can be used to begin a wider conversation. The short answers to the questions below should in no way be considered absolute but rather are intended to lead the questioner down a path for more information. The questions in this section are based on real ones that I and other Jewish colleagues have received from non-Jews looking to educate themselves about Judaism and its people. Why eighteen? Each Hebrew letter has a numerical value, and to make the number eighteen, the Hebrew letters *yud* (value of ten) and *chet* (value of eight) are required. Together, those two letters spell out the Hebrew word *Chai*, which means "life." Traditionally, the letter "eighteen" has been a symbol of good luck or the celebration of life, and gifts are given to others within multiples of eighteen. With the fullness of life, I present eighteen questions as a gift to my Christian readers.

1. Why Don't You Wear That Little Hat Thingy?

This question deserves a two-pronged answer. The first answer defines the Jewish object, and the second distinguishes between Jews of different denominations. The "hat thingy" you refer to is known as a *kippah* in Hebrew or *yarmulke* (ya-mah-kah) in Yiddish. A kippah is used as a traditional object of modesty by Jewish men and also has cultural origins, which brings us to the second part of the question. The World Council of Churches alleges that there are currently over forty thousand denominations or sects of Christianity in the world. This being the case, it would seem silly to assume that all Jews belong to the same denomination, practice the religion the same, and don the same ritual objects. The most common Jewish denominations are Orthodox Judaism, Conservative Judaism, Reform Judaism, Reconstructionist Judaism, and Humanistic Judaism, and there are differing sects, branches, and individualistic practices within each of them. While Orthodox Jewry asserts that men are required to wear a kippah at all times, other denominations say the wearing of a kippah is optional, open to men and women alike, and worn at different times. During my time as a congregational rabbi, I opted to wear a kippah during what I believed to be "spiritually charged" moments.

2. Don't We Jews and Christians Alike Worship the Same God?

As a matter of fact, no, we don't. The Jewish God, who admittedly has evolved through the course of biblical and rabbinic literature, is not the same deity as the Christian God. The Christian God, who is the "Father" part of the Trinity, exists alongside Jesus (the Son of God) and the Holy Spirit. Neither of these characters appears within the theology of God in the Jewish faith. The idea that God would be anthropomorphic and conceive a son is more akin to the mythology of the Greek and Roman gods. Moreover, the way that we "worship" is quite different. Judaism understands God's relationship with the people of Israel to be a *communal* one, and while this is present in some forms of Christianity, other forms see an *individual* connection. While there are similarities between the Jewish God and what Christians might call the Father, the differences are far too great to assert that they are the "same."

3. What Do Jews Believe about the Messiah?

The term "Messiah" comes from the Hebrew *Mashiach*, translated as "Anointed One," as kings and prophets were often "anointed" with oil in the presence of the community to denote their authority. Differing traditions exist and have existed regarding the Messiah in Judaism. Some denominations and traditions believe the Messiah to be anthropomorphic, and others believe that a messianic age without a particular messianic figure will one day come. What brings the Jewish Messiah or messianic age also differs among denominations, but in Judaism, the coming of this would bring about the Olam Haba, "the world to come," in which God and humans would unite together in peace and common worship.

4. What Do Jews Believe Happens after They Die? Do Jews Have a Heaven or Hell?

Again, Jews of differing denominations may answer differently, but truthfully, Jews don't have much to say about the afterlife. It is not a subject discussed in great detail by the sages or by modern Jews. The focus of Judaism is the life we live here and now, the concept of being moral as commanded to do so without hoping or believing in a divine reward at the end of our days. If you ask a Jew what is waiting in the next life, the answer is most likely to be "I don't know, and I don't care." This is likely foreign to most Christians who have established concepts of heaven and hell, which do not exist in Jewish theological thought. Jews do not engage in good deeds for an end goal in the next world; indeed, even the Jewish mystics believe that Jews must engage in activities in order to bring the world 90 percent of the way to perfection, and only then will God complete that perfection with the last 10 percent. Our goal is that we get to live in a better world now, not later. That being said, Orthodox Jews do have some understanding of Gehenna or Sheol, which are Jewish versions of hell and are written about in rabbinic literature, but outside of the ultra-Orthodox sects, this is seen as allegory.

5. Does Judaism Hold One Particular Theological or Political View?

Differing beliefs, law codes, and political thoughts have evolved and split over the centuries, with many Jews holding opposing views and varying theological and ritualistic understandings. Do all the followers within the thousands of denominations of Christianity believe the same things? Certainly not. Further, political views are based only partly on Jewish law and beliefs, especially by those who adhere to them, and sometimes political views stand in direct contrast with what "Judaism" might say.

6. What Is Your View on the State of Israel?

Most Jews have different opinions on the establishment, safety, and government of the State of Israel. These views have evolved since Israel's establishment in 1948. Moreover, most Jews don't enjoy speaking about Israel because the topic has become (perhaps always was) polarizing, charged, divisive, emotional, and misunderstood. Many modern Jews think of the State of Israel as family. As we all know, we love our family members unconditionally, but that doesn't mean we have to like them all the time. Some Jews take issue with the Israeli government's actions, such as the occupation and the Orthodox influence and laws, while others celebrate or defend them. The importance of the Jewish State also varies among denominations, with some having extreme views on either side and others in the middle of the spectrum. One thing is certain: it is a complicated question and an even more individualistic and complex answer.

7. Doesn't Judaism Have a "Satan" Too?

The name Satan appears in only one book of the Hebrew Bible, the book of Job, a book that has its own distinct theological viewpoints, some of which are in direct contrast with other books of the canon. In the story of Job, a character called הַשָּׂטָן (HaSatan) in Hebrew appears as an angelic being who speaks to God. HaSatan is translated as "the adversary" or "the accuser." The character is far from the Christian understanding of the devil or a fallen angel but instead conforms to a biblical belief that angels around God have specific purposes, including this one, whose purpose is to be the "prosecuting attorney," so to speak, to challenge God, such as when he asks, "Does Job not have good reason to fear God?"[1] According to Jewish thought, angels do not have free will and hence cannot do anything without God's permission; thus it was God's choice, according to this belief, to employ an angel to question God's choices. This character appears often in later rabbinic tales, such as in the midrash, but again, HaSatan is in the employment of God, per Jewish tradition, and does not imbue any "evil" characteristic.

8. So What Do Jews Think of Jesus? Where Does He Fit into Your Religion?

The best "short" answer to this question is provided by my teacher and mentor Dr. Michael Cook, who succinctly answers this about Jesus: "[He was] a charismatic Jew who felt a mission to declare that God was bringing the messianic age (the 'Kingdom of God') *soon* and taught this idea. But he was mistaken."[2] Jews do not acknowledge Jesus as a messianic figure, as he (like other messianic figures) did not bring an end to suffering or unite the world under one God and religion. We do see Jesus as a historical figure, undeniably influential, but a man who created a movement that split from first-century Judaism and became its own religion. Unfortunately, Jesus does not "fit into" the Jewish religion except through the pain and suffering experienced by Jews from the atrocities at the hands of followers of Jesus and the writings about him that followed.

9. Who Are "Jews for Jesus" and "Messianics"?

Jews for Jesus and Messianics are part of two distinct groups with different views and agendas. Most importantly, because both groups hold the belief that Jesus is the Messiah, their religions blend evangelical Christian theology with Jewish practice. They are considered not sects of Judaism but rather sects of Christianity. Jews for Jesus members have been seen to be "quasi-cultic, highly aggressive, even invasive" in their attempts to recruit Jews to convert to this brand of Christian belief.[3] While they take an active approach to conversion to Christianity, Messianics take a far more sinister and passive approach. They list their houses of worship as "synagogues," call their spiritual leaders "rabbis," and create almost indistinguishable synagogue layouts to appear Jewish. It is not until the liturgy is read that Jesus's name—in Hebrew, Yeshua—appears and the attempted conversion through subterfuge is revealed. The concept that one can "remain Jewish" while embracing Jesus is beyond absurd. By embracing a messianic figure not predestined by Jewish law or belief, the believer loses their Jewish identity. Both Christian groups, Jews for Jesus and Messianics, pose a danger to Judaism not only because of their conversion tactics but because they purposely blur the lines between Judaism and Christianity, inherently creating a revisionist history that bonds the two very different religions together.

10. When Did Judaism and Christianity Officially Split into Two Religions?

While most like to keep to what is known as the "master narrative" that Christians had severed themselves from Jews or Judaism by the end of the first century CE, the answer is far more complicated. As we have discussed, by the end of the first century CE, the Gospels had been written and the Council of Yavneh had been established. Reading the Gospels may give the impression Christians wanted nothing to do with Jews already by the end of the first century. But it is only fiction that Judaism and Christianity broke away from each other so soon after the death of Jesus. In fact, scholarship now rejects the idea that Judaism was indeed the "mother" of Christianity; rather, they remained "sister" religions for centuries, as Daniel Boyarin explains:

> At least well into late antiquity . . . Judaism and Christianity never quite formed entirely separate identities. . . . For at least the first three centuries of their common lives, Judaism in all of its forms and Christianity in all of its forms were part of one complex religious family, twins in the womb, contenting with each other for identity and precedence, but sharing to a large extent the same spiritual food. . . . It was the birth of the hegemonic Catholic Church . . . that seems finally to have precipitated the consolidation of rabbinic Judaism as Jewish

orthodoxy. . . . Then Judaism and Christianity finally emerged
from the womb as genuinely independent children of Rebecca.[4]

In other words, the first three centuries of the Common Era
were more akin to the postmodern world of religion we see
today, with different variations of denominations of Judaism
and Christianity forming hybrid identities and having their own
problems with authorities. It was not until the two institutions,
the Christian church and the Jewish Orthodoxy, were established that the ties were finally severed.

11. Does Judaism Hold a Concept of "Sin" and Forgiveness for Those Sins?

Yes, Judaism does have a concept of sin. The word for "sin" in
Hebrew is *hatat*, which shares the root with a word seen in Judges
20:16: "Of all this force—700 picked men—were left-handed.
Every one of them could sling a stone at a hair and not **miss**"
(my emphasis). The word for "miss" in this verse is where we Jews
understand the meaning of "sin," which is "missing the mark" or
"missing the target." In other words, to sin in Judaism is to make
a mistake and stray from the life we attempt to live. It does not
hold the same weight as the concept of sinning in Christianity. That being said, sin is taken seriously in Judaism, and it is
addressed each year during the High Holy Day observances of
Rosh Hashanah (the Jewish New Year) and Yom Kippur (the
Day of Atonement). It is within these days (and the surrounding Jewish month) that Jews are commanded to think about the
sins they have committed over the past year and attempt to correct them. In Jewish tradition, a Jew is commanded to seek forgiveness from God, which is done not only through the Yom
Kippur liturgy but also to see forgiveness from sins committed against fellow human beings. The Mishnah describes this

in Yoma 8:9: "Furthermore, for transgressions between a person and God, Yom Kippur atones; however, for transgressions between a person and another, Yom Kippur does not atone until he appeases the other person."[5] The sin is forgiven when Jews make what is known as *teshuvah*, "turning." A Jew corrects behavior by turning toward the right path, asking for forgiveness, and vowing to change the behavior that led to the sin.

12. Is It Possible to Be Jewish and Not Believe in God?

Yes, but this question addresses a few aspects of Judaism. My first response is that there exists a denomination of Judaism called Humanistic, which expresses a Judaism "independent of a supernatural authority."[6] The Society for Humanistic Judaism states that "secular Humanistic Judaism is a movement within Judaism and one of five recognized Jewish denominations. It combines Jewish meaning and culture with a human-centered philosophy of life. It defines Judaism as the historical and cultural experience of the Jewish people while affirming that people are independent of supernatural authority and responsible for themselves and their behavior."[7]

My second response has to do with "secular" or "nonpracticing" Jews, who focus on the cultural or ethnic link to Judaism. Many Jews in the world, even in Israel, see their Judaism not as a religious practice but as part of their ethnic or cultural identity. For these Jews, belief in God, therefore, is not necessary. Finally, Judaism teaches that research and exploration of belief are encouraged, and blind faith is to be avoided. Therefore, questioning the existence of God and discovering a belief that fits the individual Jew perfectly is not only accepted but encouraged. Judaism holds countless ideas about God, and finding your own meaning or acceptance of God is a journey that all Jews take, even if part of that journey is a time when the existence of God is questioned.

13. Does the Concept of "Grace" Exist in Judaism?

Grace, according to Christian theology, is "the spontaneous, unmerited gift of the divine favour in the salvation of sinners, and the divine influence operating in individuals for their regeneration and sanctification."[8] Most understand it to be an undeserved divine gift of unconditional love to those who have faith in Jesus as both the Messiah and Savior, a meaning that comes from Romans 3:23–26 and Ephesians 2:8–9. That being said, Judaism does recognize God's love, though quite differently. Jewish tradition teaches that God showed the Jewish people love by providing the Torah, a way to live morally, and Jews show love to God by following the commandments within the Torah.

14. Can We Share the Gospel with Jews?

Jews recognize that it is part of the Christian ethos to "spread the good news" of the gospel to Jews and others. That being said, Jews can (and often do) find it invasive and disturbing when Christians proselytize, especially when concepts such as consent are ignored. Jews do not feel that we are "missing" anything or are "incomplete," nor do we feel that we need to be "fulfilled." Moreover, proselytizing to Jews brings up a collective PTSD from Jewish history, when Christians not only proselytized to Jews but tried to forcibly convert them, at times under the threat of torture and death. A good rule to follow, therefore, is to remember these things when approaching a Jew and listen to the answer a Jew gives to the offer. If the answer is no, we ask that Christians respect that answer and move on. To continue in the face of a no disregards consent and brings out the PTSD as spoken about above. Additionally, when Jews and Christians engage in dialogue for understanding, we Jews ask that Christians refrain from proselytizing at the "table," so to speak, to show respect. Unfortunately, Jews have encountered situations in which interfaith dialogue was just a "cover" for proselytizing and conversion.

15. Doesn't the "Suffering Servant" Point to Jesus in Isaiah 53?

Within the Jewish historical context, the answer is no. As Robert Alter states, "Virtually no serious scholars today see this as a prediction of the Passion, but it certainly provided a theological template for interpreting the death of Jesus."[9] Jews do not see the context of the Isaiah texts as having to do with Jesus at all but rather see the identity of the servant as the collective Israel and that "the nations are stunned that such an insignificant and lowly group turns out to have been so important to the divine plan."[10] Other commentators, such as Abraham Ibn Ezra, see the servant character to be Isaiah himself, with the speaker as one of Isaiah's disciples. Other theories suggest the speaker is Judean and "the servant is either a pious minority (the ideal Israel, in contrast to the mass of Judeans whose faith and behavior miss the mark God set for them) or some individual within the Israelite community."[11] In the end, Jews do not believe the prophets are "pointing" to a future messianic character of any sort, and their messages were intended for the historical contexts in which they lived.

16. What about Isaiah 7:14? If It Does Not Point to Jesus, to Whom Does It Point?

Earlier in this volume, we discussed the translation issue with "young girl" and "virgin," but the crux of the issue also involves that of the identity of Immanuel, translated as "God is with us." If not Jesus, to whom does it point in Jewish tradition? Rashi, a twelfth-century commentator, states that the name refers to

> our Rock shall be with us, and this is the sign, for she is a young girl, and she never prophesied, yet in this instance, Divine inspiration shall rest upon her. This is what is stated below (8:3): "And I was intimate with the prophetess, etc.," and we do not find a prophet's wife called a prophetess unless she prophesied. Some interpret this as being said about Hezekiah, but it is impossible, because, when you count his years, you find that Hezekiah was born nine years before his father's reign. And some interpret that this is the sign, that she was a young girl and incapable of giving birth.[12]

However, modern commentators and scholars understand the name Immanuel to represent a sign of the times and that "God is with Judah, both to protect it . . . and to punish it."[13] In other words, the birth points not to someone in the future but to the present situation in which Isaiah is living and preaching.

17. Why Weren't the Apocrypha and Pseudepigrapha Included in the Hebrew Bible Canon?

According to modern scholars, the Hebrew Bible was canonized over a long period of time, with most sections, such as the Torah and the Prophets, accepted before the first century CE. However, by the end of the first century CE, aspects of the Hebrew Bible were still fluid and not set in stone, such as the books "Song of Songs, Ecclesiastes, and Esther."[14] When the apocryphal books were being composed, it was during the time when there already were limits on canonization, and thus they were most likely not included in the canon because of these restrictions. However, it is probable that while the books of the Apocrypha were not included in the final canon, they were regarded as divine or divinely inspired by certain circles of first-century Judaism. There is also the added aspect that most of the apocryphal books are written in Greek, not Hebrew, and would not fit in an otherwise Hebrew canon.

18. What Is It You'd Like Christians to Take Away from This Book as a Whole?

Certain common questions, such as those above or those raised in earlier chapters, are asked of Jews, sometimes respectfully and sometimes not. My hope is that Christian clergy and others who wish to provide real insights into these matters will help their congregations ask the proper questions in the correct way and teach them how to accept and perhaps engage in friendly dialogue. The more attuned your congregants are to these questions and answers, the more accurately they can pass this information on to others and "pay it forward" to other Christians in your community, thus reducing the opportunities for ignorance and misunderstandings regarding the Jewish religion. If hate is the child of ignorance, then asking these questions and having the correct answers can only assist in the fight for fruitful interreligious dialogue and acts of social justice and eventually, we can hope, the bettering of our world.

There are, of course, more questions to ask. Find a local rabbi and write down your questions as you think of them. Ask them out of genuine curiosity, and you will find yourself at the desk of a resource who wishes to help you better the relationship between Jews and Christians.

Acknowledgments

Many thanks to those whose work, research, and support helped me write this book, including the words of Dr. Michael Cook, Dr. Amy Jill-Levine, Dr. Marc Brettler, Dr. Daniel Boyarin, Dr. David Sandmel, Dr. Dean Bell, Bishop John Shelby Spong, and many more giants upon whose shoulders I am able to stand. I am grateful to the libraries of Hebrew Union College–Jewish Institute of Religion, Spertus Institute of Jewish Learning and Leadership, Purdue University, and Xavier University for the wealth of knowledge and resources found therein. I am especially thankful to my seminary professors at Hebrew Union College–Jewish Institute of Religion, who pushed me to hone my writing and research skills and taught me to think critically, most notably Dr. David H. Aaron and Dr. Gary P. Zola.

I also cannot neglect the others who helped this book come about, such as friends and family who held patience for me in writing it and allowed me to vent about the difficulty of the process—some even dared to look at a few pages in light of their busy schedules. I am very appreciative. I am especially thankful for my ex-wife, Barrie, who, throughout many years as a congregational rabbi, suffered through reading and editing my hundreds of sermons and newsletters, thus shaping me by her comments into a better writer. And while I know my children would've preferred I write a comic book (as they have often told me), it is my hope that they know how much their love sustained me during this process.

I am eternally thankful to and humbled by all who have, in ways big and small, played a part in this book coming to be. It, indeed, takes a village.

Notes

Introduction

1 Luke 13:11.
2 Luke 13:14.
3 Luke 13:15–16.
4 *Nostra aetate*, Latin for "In our time," refers to the document "Declaration on the Relation of the Church to Non-Christian Religions" by the Second Vatican Council, October 28, 1965. The document changed the church's approach to Jews after nearly two thousand years of pain and sorrow. It repudiates the centuries-old "deicide" charge against all Jews, stresses the bond shared by Jews and Catholics, and dismisses the church's interest in trying to baptize Jews.
5 John Shelby Spong, speech at the Chautauqua Institution, 2012.

Chapter 1: Let's Right a Few Wrongs

1 Michael Cook, *Modern Jews Engage the New Testament: Enhancing Jewish Well-Being in a Christian Environment* (Woodstock, VT: Jewish Lights, 2008), 24.
2 James Carroll, *Constantine's Sword: The Church and the Jews, a History* (New York: Houghton, Mifflin Harcourt, 2001), 116.
3 Norman Gottwald, *The Hebrew Bible: A Socio-literary Introduction* (Philadelphia: Fortress, 1985), 7.

4 Gottwald, 7.

5 Luke 1:4.

6 Cook, *Modern Jews*, 195.

7 Cook, 196.

8 Deuteronomy 6:4.

9 Cook, *Modern Jews*, 197.

10 Lamentations 1:5.

11 Lawrence Schiffman, *From Text to Tradition: A History of Judaism in Second Temple and Rabbinic Times* (Hoboken, NJ: Ktav, 1991), 33.

12 Schiffman, 62.

13 Schiffman, 73.

14 Schiffman, 98.

15 Samuel Sandmel, *A Jewish Understanding of the New Testament* (Woodstock, VT: Jewish Lights, 2004), 24–25.

16 Dean Phillip Bell, ed., *The Bloomsbury Companion to Jewish Studies* (New York: Bloomsbury Academic, 2015), 363.

17 "Josephus: Antiquities of the Jews, Book XVIII," penelope .uchicago.edu, accessed January 27, 2022, http://penelope .uchicago.edu/josephus/ant-18.html; see chapter 1, point 3.

18 Gary Porton, "The World of the Rabbis," in Bell, *Bloomsbury Companion*, 59.

19 Daniel Boyarin, *The Jewish Gospels: The Story of the Jewish Christ* (New York: New Press, 2012), xii–xiv.

20 Daniel Boyarin, *Border Lines: The Partition of Judaeo-Christianity* (Philadelphia: University of Pennsylvania Press, 2012), 58.

21 Cook, *Modern Jews*, 44.

22 Gottwald, *Hebrew Bible*, 6.

23 Porton, "World of the Rabbis," 59.

24 Porton, 59.

25 Porton, 59.

26 Roland Deines, "Biblical Views: The Pharisees—Good Guys with Bad Press," *Biblical Archaeology Review* 39, no. 4 (July/August 2013), https://www.baslibrary.org/biblical-archaeology-review/39/4/8.

27 Matthew 23:13–36.

28 Boyarin, *Jewish Gospels*, xv.

29 Matthew 12:1–21.

30 Kurt Skelly, "10 Marks of a Pharisee," Ministry127, accessed January 27, 2022, https://ministry127.com/christian-living/10-marks-of-a-pharisee.

31 Sandmel, *Jewish Understanding*, 30.

32 Cook, *Modern Jews*, 49.

33 Mark 14:53–65.

34 Matthew 26:64–67.

35 Cook, *Modern Jews*, 42.

36 Cook, 48.

37 Schiffman, *From Text to Tradition*, 152.

38 Amy-Jill Levine and Marc Zvi Brettler, eds., *The Jewish Annotated New Testament* (New York: Oxford University Press, 2017), 91.

39 Michael D. Coogan, ed., *The Oxford History of the Biblical World* (New York: Oxford University Press, 2001), 386.

40 Porton, "World of the Rabbis," 61.

41 Cook, *Modern Jews*, xix.

42 Cook, xix.

43 Porton, "World of the Rabbis," 65.

44 Porton, 65.

45 James Kugel, "The Irreconcilability of Judaism and Modern Biblical Scholarship," *Studies in Bible and Antiquity* 8, article 3 (2016): 14, https://scholarsarchive.byu.edu/cgi/viewcontent.cgi?article=1057&context=sba.

46 Kugel, 17.

47 Schiffman, *From Text to Tradition*, 181.

48 Pirkei Avot 1.4, trans. Dr. Joshua Kulp, Sefaria, accessed December 20, 2021, https://www.sefaria.org/Pirkei_Avot.1.4 ?lang=bi&with=all&lang2=en.

49 Pirkei Avot 1.4 (brackets in the original).

50 Pirkei Avot 1.4 (brackets in the original).

51 Pirkei Avot 1.4 (brackets in the original).

52 Coogan, *Oxford History*, 386.

Chapter 2: Avoiding the Land Mines

1   Michael Harvey, "The Limits of Communication," Reform Judaism, accessed January 27, 2022, https://reformjudaism.org/ learning/torah-study/torah-commentary/limits-communication.

2   Edward F. Campbell, "A Land Divided: Judah and Israel from the Death of Solomon to the Fall of Samaria," in *The Oxford History of the Biblical World* (New York: Oxford University Press, 1998), 239.

3   Campbell, 239.

4   2 Kings 17:24 (brackets in the original).

5   Sandmel, *Jewish Understanding*, 179.

6   Luke 10:25–37.

7   Levine and Brettler, *Jewish Annotated New Testament*, 123.

8   Sifra Kedoshim 4, trans. Rabbi Shraga Silverstein, Sefaria, accessed December 21, 2021, https://www.sefaria.org/Sifra%2C _Kedoshim%2C_Chapter_4.12?lang=bi&with=all&lang2=e.

9   Luke 10:31–32.

10 Matthew 27:24–25.

11 Cook, *Modern Jews*, 129.

12 John Shelby Spong, *The Sins of Scripture: Exposing the Bible's Texts of Hate to Reveal the God of Love* (San Francisco: Harper-One, 2006), 185.

13 Matthew 27:25.

14 Levine and Brettler, *Jewish Annotated New Testament*, 52.

15 Tord Fornberg, "Deicide and Genocide: Matthew, the Death of Jesus, and Auschwitz," *Svensk Exegetisk Årsbok* 61 (1996): 97.

16 Levine and Brettler, *Jewish Annotated New Testament*, 84.

17 Levine and Brettler, 85.

18 Matthew 21:38–39.

19 John 8:44.

20 Cook, *Modern Jews*, 129.

21 Cook, 125.

22 Carroll, *Constantine's Sword*, 87.

23 Cook, *Modern Jews*, 125.

24 Eric Werner, "Melito of Sardes, the First Poet of Deicide," *Hebrew Union College Annual* 37 (1966): 193.

25 Urban C. Von Wahlde, "The References to the Time and Place of the Crucifixion in the *Peri Pascha* of Melito of Sardis," *Journal of Theological Studies* 60, no. 2 (2009): 556, https://doi.org/10.1093/jts/flp092.

26 Werner, "Melito of Sardes," 192.

27 Werner, 193.

28 Some of this section comes from *Nostra aetate* and Michael E. Harvey, "Abiding Response: The Case of Fifty-Years of Graduates of the Hebrew Union College-Jewish Institute of Religion" (master's thesis, Hebrew Union College-Jewish Institute of Religion, 2015).

29 Pope Paul VI, "Declaration on the Relation of the Church to Non-Christian Religions," Vatican, 1965, http://www.vatican.va/archive/hist_councils/ii_vatican_council/documents/vat-ii_decl_19651028_nostra-aetate_en.html.

30 Pope Paul VI; some of this section comes from *Nostra aetate* and Harvey, "Abiding Response."

31 Werner, "Melito of Sardes," 192.

32 Rita Ferrone, "Anti-Jewish Elements in the Extraordinary Form," *Worship* 84, no. 6 (2010): 2.

33 Carroll, *Constantine's Sword*, 42.

34 Ferrone, "Anti-Jewish Elements."

35 "The 1662 Book of Common Prayer," justus.anglican.org, accessed January 27, 2022, http://justus.anglican.org/resources/bcp/1662/baskerville.htm.

36 "1662 Book of Common Prayer."

37 Ferrone, "Anti-Jewish Elements," 20.

38 Susannah Heschel, "Something Holy in a Profane Place: Germans and Jews in Suffering and Prayer," *Christianity and Crisis* 46, no. 14 (1986): 342.

39 Wikipedia, s.v. "Christianese," last modified November 14, 2021, 01:39, https://en.wikipedia.org/wiki/Christianese.

40 C. Michael Patton, "Learning to Speak like a Christian: 40 Examples of Christianese," Credo House Ministries, July 13, 2021, https://credohouse.org/blog/learning-to-speak-like-a -christian-40-examples-of-christianese.

41 Cook, *Modern Jews*, 258.

42 Cook, 258.

43 David Goldman, "Why We Can't Hear Wagner's Music," *First Things*, December 2010, https://www.firstthings.com/article/2010/12/why-we-cant-hear-wagners-music.

44 Goldman.

45 W. Reeves, "Das Judenthum In Der Musik," Open Library, 1910, https://openlibrary.org/books/OL7019739M/Judaism_in_music.

46 Goldman, "Wagner's Music" (brackets in the original).

47 James Loeffler, "Richard Wagner's 'Jewish Music': Antisemitism and Aesthetics in Modern Jewish Culture," *Jewish Social Studies* 15, no. 2 (Winter 2009), https://doi.org/10.2979/jss.2009.15.2.2.

48 Sammy Saltzman, "Jews Responsible for All 'Wars in the World,' but Mel Gibson Not Responsible for DUI Anymore," CBS News, October 7, 2009, https://www.cbsnews.com/news/

jews-responsible-for-all-wars-in-the-world-but-mel-gibson
-not-responsible-for-dui-anymore/.

Chapter 3: So Much to Celebrate

1   Exodus 12:13; my emphasis.
2   "Blood Libel: A False, Incendiary Claim against Jews," Anti-
    Defamation League, accessed January 27, 2022, https://www
    .adl.org/education/resources/glossary-terms/blood-libel.
3   "Blood Libel."
4   *Gravette Herald*, April 23, 1997, quoted in Cook, *Modern Jews*,
    110.
5   Cook, *Modern Jews*, 109.
6   As quoted in Jonathan Klawans, "Jesus' Last Supper Still Wasn't
    a Passover Seder Meal," Biblical Archaeology Society, Febru-
    ary 12, 2016, https://www.biblicalarchaeology.org/daily/people
    -cultures-in-the-bible/jesus-historical-jesus/jesus-last-supper
    -passover-seder-meal/.
7   Joel Marcus, "Passover and Last Supper Revisited," *New Tes-
    tament Studies* 59, no. 3 (2013): 310, https://doi.org/10.1017/
    s0028688513000076.
8   Cook, *Modern Jews*, 109.
9   R. Kendall Soulen, *The God of Israel and Christian Theology*
    (Minneapolis: Fortress, 1996).
10 Soulen, 181.
11 Mark 14:12.
12 Numbers 9:1–3.
13 Robert Alter, *The Hebrew Bible: A Translation with Commentary*
    (New York: W. W. Norton, 2018), 379.
14 Cook, *Modern Jews*, 111.
15 Cook, 119.
16 Jonathan Klawans, "Was Jesus' Last Supper a Seder?," Bibli-
    cal Archaeology Society, October 2001, https://www.biblical

archaeology.org/daily/people-cultures-in-the-bible/jesus -historical-jesus/was-jesus-last-supper-a-seder/.

17 Some aspects of this section are from Rabbi Harvey, "What Do We Do about Christian Seders?," *The Blogs—Michael Harvey* (blog), *Times of Israel*, April 5, 2020, https://blogs.timesofisrael .com/what-do-we-do-about-christian-seders/.

18 "Maccabees: History," Sefaria, accessed January 27, 2022, https://www.sefaria.org/topics/maccabees?tab=sheets.

19 1 Maccabees 4:42–59, Brenton's Septuagint, Sefaria, accessed December 21, 2021, https://www.sefaria.org/sheets/285839.1 ?lang=bi&with=Translations&lang2=en.

20 Zvi Ron, "Antecedents of the Hanukkah Oil Story," *Review of Rabbinic Judaism* 18, no. 1 (2015): 67.

21 Brian C. Dennert, "Hanukkah and the Testimony of Jesus' Works (John 10:22–39)," *Journal of Biblical Literature* 132, no. 2 (2013): 437.

22 Victor J. Donovan, "Hanukkah and Christmas," *Worship* 31, no. 1 (2013): 45.

23 "Christian-Jewish Relations: Burning of the Talmud," Jewish Virtual Library, accessed January 24, 2022, https://www .jewishvirtuallibrary.org/burning-of-the-talmud.

24 Some of this section is from Rabbi Harvey, "You Take Christmas, I'll Take Hanukkah," *The Blogs—Michael Harvey* (blog), *Times of Israel*, December 10, 2020, https://blogs.timesofisrael .com/you-take-christmas-ill-take-hanukkah/.

25 Yael Shahar, "Where Did Shavuot Come From? Hint: Not the Torah," *Haaretz*, May 20, 2015, https://www.haaretz.com/ jewish/.premium-where-shavuot-comes-from-1.5364483.

26 Exodus 23:14–16.

27 Numbers 28:26.

28 "Mishnah Bikkurim 3:1," Sefaria, accessed January 24, 2022, https://www.sefaria.org/Mishnah_Bikkurim.3.1?lang=bi& with=all&lang2=en.

29 "Shavuot History," Reform Judaism, accessed January 24, 2022, https://reformjudaism.org/jewish-holidays/shavuot/shavuot -history.

30 Shahar, "Where Did Shavuot Come From?"

31 Acts 2:1–4.

32 John 7:1–5.

33 "The Things We Have in Common," February 19, 1939, Ferdinand M. Isserman Papers, MS-6, box 15, folder 4, American Jewish Archives, Cincinnati, OH.

34 Parts of this section are from Rabbi Harvey, "Interfaith Sermon—St. John's Episcopal Church," rabbiharvey.wordpress .com, November 11, 2018, https://rabbiharvey.wordpress.com/ 2018/11/11/interfaith-sermon-st-johns-episcopal-church-11 -11-18/.

35 For example, Josh Mandel (@JoshMandelOhio), "America was founded and grew strong on a bedrock of Judeo-Christian values," Twitter, March 21, 2021, https://twitter.com/Josh MandelOhio/status/1411378503434579968.

36 James Loeffler, "The Problem with the 'Judeo-Christian Tradition,'" *Atlantic*, August 1, 2020, https://www.theatlantic.com/ ideas/archive/2020/08/the-judeo-christian-tradition-is-over/ 614812.

37 M. J. C. Warren, "Why 'Judeo-Christian Values' Are a Dog-Whistle Myth Peddled by the Far Right," Conversation, November 7, 2017, https://theconversation.com/why-judeo -christian-values-are-a-dog-whistle-myth-peddled-by-the-far -right-85922.

38 Rabbi Danya Ruttenberg (@TheRaDR), "'Judeo-Christian' isn't a thing. It a) positions Jews & Christians against Muslims, is Islamophobic b) elides Christian oppression & murder of Jews," Twitter, January 27, 2019, https://twitter.com/ TheRaDR/status/1089589999920660484.

39 Warren, "Judeo-Christian Values."

40 Loeffler, "Judeo-Christian Tradition."

41 Wikipedia, s.v. "Judeo-Christian," last modified January 6, 2022, 00:12, https://en.wikipedia.org/wiki/Judeo-Christian.

42 "ILGL Statement on Biblical Literacy," Interfaith Leaders of Greater Lafayette, March 3, 2019, https://interfaithleadersgl .home.blog/2019/03/03/ilgl-statement-on-biblical-literacy -march-2019.

43 Matthew 7:12.

44 Talmud Bavli, Shabbat 31a.

45 Some of this section is from Rabbi Harvey, "'Interfaith Dialogue'—Sermon at Vesper Service for Westminster," rabbi harvey.wordpress.com, February 25, 2018, https://rabbiharvey .wordpress.com/2018/02/25/interfaith-dialogue-sermon-at -vesper-service-for-westminster/.

46 Matthew 7:9–12.

47 Boyarin, *Border Lines*, 44.

Chapter 4: The Difference in Our Canons

1 Gary Rendsburg, "Israel without the Bible," in *The Hebrew Bible: New Insights and Scholarship*, ed. Frederick E. Green- spahn (New York: New York University Press, 2008), 3–23.

2 Rendsburg, 7.

3 Alexander Fantalkin and Oren Tal, "The Canonization of the Pentateuch: When and Why? (Part II)," *Zeitschrift Für Die Alttestamentliche Wissenschaft* 124, no. 2 (2012): 212, https://doi .org/10.1515/zaw-2012-0015.

4 Gerald T. Sheppard, "Canonization: Hearing the Voice of the Same God through Historically Dissimilar Traditions," *Inter- pretation* 36, no. 1 (1982): 26.

5 Philip R. Davies, *Scribes and Schools: The Canonization of the Hebrew Scriptures* (Louisville, KY: Westminster John Knox, 1998), 95.

6 Numbers 36:10–13.

7 Numbers 27:15–23.

8 Numbers 27:12–14.

9 Sheppard, "Canonization," 27.

10 John Van Seters, *The Pentateuch: A Social-Science Commentary* (New York: Bloomsbury Academic, 1999), 101–2.

11 Michael R. Greenwald, "The Canon of the New Testament," in Levine and Brettler, *Jewish Annotated New Testament*, 559.

12 Aaron, David H. *Etched in Stone: The Emergence of the Decalogue*, (T & T Clark, 2006), 15, 181.

13 Genesis 12:10–12 JPS and my translation.

14 Genesis 20:1–18 JPS and my translation.

15 S. David Sperling, *The Original Torah: The Political Intent of the Bible's Writers* (New York: New York University Press, 1998), 23.

16 Sperling, 23.

17 Sheppard, "Canonization," 25.

18 Norman K. Gottwald, *The Hebrew Bible: A Brief Socio-literary Introduction* (Minneapolis: Fortress, 2008), 73.

19 Gottwald, 73.

20 Levine and Brettler, *Jewish Annotated New Testament*, 560.

21 This table is based on Gottwald, *Hebrew Bible*, 60–61.

22 Genesis 1:1.

23 Exodus 1:1.

Chapter 5: Translation and Typology

1 "File:Tikkun-Koreim-HB50656.pdf," Wikimedia Commons, accessed January 24, 2022, https://commons.wikimedia.org/wiki/File:Tikkun-Koreim-HB50656.pdf.

2 Exodus 23:19; 34:26; Deuteronomy 14:21.

3 Exodus 23:18; my emphasis.

4 Some parts of this section are from Rabbi Harvey, "'Chalav or Chaylev?,'" rabbiharvey.wordpress.com, May 20, 2016, https://rabbiharvey.wordpress.com/2016/05/20/chalev-or-chaylev/.

5 Exodus 18:11.

6 The NRSV translation includes the note "The clause *because . . . Egyptians* has been transposed from verse 10."

7 John A. Simpson, *The Oxford English Dictionary* (Oxford: Clarendon Press, 1991), 3984.

8 Frederick E. Greenspahn, *Hapax Legomena in Biblical Hebrew: A Study of the Phenomenon and Its Treatment since Antiquity with Special Reference to Verbal Forms*, SBL Dissertation Series 74 (Chico, CA: Scholars, 1984), 29.

9 Bold and italics are my emphasis.

10 Deuteronomy 14:16.

11 David Bellos, *Is That a Fish in Your Ear? Translation and the Meaning of Everything* (New York: Farrar, Straus and Giroux, 2011), 159.

12 Alan Sheridan, *Michel Foucault: The Will to Truth* (London: Routledge, 1980), 94.

13 Isaiah 7:14; my emphasis.

14 Isaiah 7:14; my emphasis.

15 Genesis 24:43; my emphasis.

16 Exodus 2:8; my emphasis.

17 "Isaiah 7:14," Sefaria, accessed January 27, 2022, https://www.sefaria.org/Isaiah.7.14?lang=bi&with=Rashi&lang2=en (brackets in the original).

18 John 8:44.

19 Deuteronomy 32:8–9.

20 Genesis 36:31.

21 My translation.

22 Frank E. Eakin Jr., *The Religion and Culture of Israel: An Introduction to Old Testament Thought* (Boston: Allyn and Bacon, 1971), 70.

23 Exodus 15:11; my translation.

24 Micah 4:5; my translation.

25 Joel 4:10.

26 Karri Holley, "A Cultural Repertoire of Practices in Doctoral Education," *International Journal of Doctoral Studies* 6 (2011): 80, https://doi.org/10.28945/1430.

27 Holley, 80.

28 Michel Foucault, *The Archaeology of Knowledge* (London: Routledge, 2002), 22.

29 Cook, *Modern Jews*, 259.

30 Cook, 259.

31 Isaiah 7:14.

32 Theopedia, s.v. "Biblical typology," accessed January 27, 2022, https://www.theopedia.com/biblical-typology.

33 "Zechariah 9:9," Sefaria, accessed January 27, 2022, https://www.sefaria.org/Zechariah.9.9?lang=bi&with=Rashi&lang2=en.

34 "Sanhedrin 98A:13," Sefaria, accessed January 27, 2022, https://www.sefaria.org/Sanhedrin.98a.13?lang=bi.

35 John 12:12–15.

36 Zechariah 13:7, Tanakh: The Holy Scriptures (JPS), Sefaria, accessed December 21, 2021, https://www.sefaria.org/Zechariah.13.7?lang=bi&with=all&lang2=en.

37 Mark 14:27.

38 Mark 14:28–31.

39 Zechariah 11:12–13.

40 Matthew 27:6–10.

41 This table is from Cook, *Modern Jews*, 88.

42 This information was compiled by Cook, 194. For the infancy narrative, see Matthew 1, 2; Exodus 1:1–2:10. For the wilderness temptation, see Matthew 4:1–11; Exodus 16:1–17:7. For the giving of the law, see Matthew 5, 6, 7; Exodus 19:1–23:23. For a transfiguration on a mountain, see Matthew 17:1–9; Exodus 34:29–35.

43 Isaiah 53:1–5.

44 Adele Berlin and Marc Zvi Brettler, eds., *The Jewish Study Bible* (New York: Oxford University Press, 2015), 891.

45 Berlin and Brettler, 891.

46 Jeremiah 10:18–24; 11:19.

47 Sotah 14a, William Davidson Edition, Sefaria, accessed December 21, 2021, https://www.sefaria.org/Sotah.14a.9?lang=bi& with=all&lang2=en.

48 "Isaiah 53," christianity.com, accessed January 27, 2022, https:// www.christianity.com/bible/niv/isaiah/53.

49 Wikipedia, s.v. "Smooth Criminal," last modified January 21, 2022, 02:53, https://en.wikipedia.org/wiki/Smooth_Criminal #Charts_2.

50 "Smooth Criminal."

Chapter 6: Easy Answers to Eighteen Big Questions

1 Job 1:9.

2 Cook, *Modern Jews*, 259.

3 Cook, 261.

4 Porton, "World of the Rabbis," 75.

5 Mishnah Yoma 8:9, William Davidson Edition, Sefaria, accessed December 21, 2021, https://www.sefaria.org/Mishnah _Yoma.8.9?lang=bi&with=all&lang2=en.

6 Society for Humanistic Judaism (website), accessed January 27, 2022, https://shj.org/.

7 "Humanistic Judaism FAQ," Society for Humanistic Judaism, July 13, 2021, https://shj.org/meaning-learning/what-is -humanistic-judaism/humanistic-judaism-faq/.

8 Encyclopedia Britannica, s.v. "Grace," accessed January 27, 2022, https://www.britannica.com/topic/grace-religion.

9 Robert Alter, "The Prophets," in *The Hebrew Bible: A Translation with Commentary* (New York: W. W. Norton, 2019), 801.

10 Benjamin D. Sommer, "Isaiah 53," in Berlin and Brettler, *Jewish Study Bible*, 891.

11 Berlin and Brettler, 891.

12 "Isaiah 7:14," Sefaria, accessed January 27, 2022, https://www
.sefaria.org/Isaiah.7.14?lang=bi&with=Rashi&lang2=en.

13 Benjamin D. Sommer, "Isaiah 7," in Berlin and Brettler, *Jewish
Study Bible*, 799.

14 James H. Charlesworth, "Introduction for the General Reader,"
in *The Old Testament Pseudepigrapha* (Peabody, MA: Hendrick-
son, 2016), xxiii.

General Index

Scripture Index

CPSIA information can be obtained
at www.ICGtesting.com
Printed in the USA
LVHW081625120722
723335LV00015B/690